BOOK H
READING FOR CONCEPTS

"Today is not yesterday."   Carlyle

BOOK H
READING

FOR CONCEPTS

Third Edition

Phoenix Learning Resources
New York

Reading for Concepts
Third Edition
Book H

Contributing Authors for the Reading for Concepts Series
Linda Barton, feature writer for *St. Louis Today*
Roberta H. Berry, elementary school teacher, writer
Barbara Broeking, journalist and educational publications editor
Eth Clifford, author of many volumes of fiction and poetry for youth
Ellen Dolan, juvenile book author
Barbara R. Frey, Professor of Education, State University College, Buffalo, N.Y.
Ruth Harley, author and editor of young people's periodicals
Phyllis W. Kirk, children's book editor
Richard Kirk, author of science, social studies, and reading books for youth
Thomas D. Mantel, attorney and juvenile author
Marilyn F. Peachin, journalist and editor
James N. Rogers, author-editor of science and social studies resource books
James J. Pflaum, author and editor of current events periodicals
Gloria S. Rosenzweig, writer of children's books
Jean Shirley, author of juvenile books
Rosemary Winebrenner, editor of children's books
Jean White, journalist and writer of young people's reference materials

Vocabulary
Cynthia Merman, Reading and Language Specialist

Project Management and Production
Kane Publishing Services, Inc.

Cover Design
Pencil Point Studios

Text Design
Jim Darby

Illustrators
James Cummings; Portia Takajian, GAI; Wayne Still

ISBN 0–7915–2110-9

2 3 4 5 6 7 8 9 0 05 04 03 02 01

TABLE OF CONTENTS

Purpose

This book is one of eight in the series "Reading for Concepts." It was designed to provide an opportunity for young readers to grow in reading experience while exploring a wide variety of ideas contained in the major academic disciplines.

Four basic underlying concepts are reflected in this book. They are: *Change may produce unexpected results; Some changes are planned, others are accidental; Modern ways of life require planned change; Where might change take us?* The overriding concept in this book relates to elements of creativity and exciting possibilities for the future. To illustrate these concepts, stories have been written around intriguing pieces of information that reflect these ideas. Content has been drawn from disciplines of art, history, space, biology, economics, engineering, Earth science, anthropology, mathematics, and geography. In this way, a wide array of content for meeting various interests is assured.

A narrative follows stories 20, 40, and 60. The narratives, largely drawn from folk literature, will provide a change of pace and are "just for fun" types of stories.

Teaching Procedure

Detailed suggestions for presenting the selections in this book will be found on pages 15 and 16 in the Teacher's Guide. Difficult words, with grade-level definitions, are listed by story on pages 6-12. Important content-area proper nouns not defined in the text are included in this listing.

Following each article is a test, which is especially designed to improve specific skills in reading. The test items were created to incorporate the thinking skills reflected in Benjamin S. Bloom's *Taxonomy of Educational Objectives*, which is explained on pages 6-7 in the Teacher's Guide.

Concept Recapitulations

After students have completed each of the three sections of this book, you may conduct a discussion to tie together the information carried in the individual articles in terms of the overall concept. Guiding questions are found on page 13 for Concept I, page 57 for Concept II, page 101 for Concept III, and page 145 for Concept IV.

Have a few priming possibilities ready to suggest, or shape them out of earlier offerings from the group. Sophisticated statements and a review of specifics are not to be expected. Look for signs of mental play and the movement of information from one setting to another. It is perfectly reasonable to conclude with unanswered questions for students to ponder in retrospect. However, it is important to give students the satisfaction of enthusiastic acceptance of their early attempts at this type

STEPS FOR THE READER

A. Turn to page 14. Look at the picture. Read the title. Think about what the story will say.

B. Study the words for this page on the list beginning on page 6.

C. Read the story carefully.

D. Put your name and the title of the story on a sheet of paper.

Number from one to nine. Begin the test on the page next to the story.

1. This question asks you to remember something the story has told you. Which of the four choices is correct for this sentence?

2. The question asks you to find the word in the story that means the same as the words in italics. The question gives you a paragraph number. Read that part again to be sure you have the right word.

3. Reread the paragraph given. Which word is described by the words given in the question? The given words must modify or explain the word or words you select.

4. This question wants you to think about the story. The answer is not in your book. Read the choices. Choose the one that is the very best guess you might make from the ideas you have just read.

5. The question tests your memory for a detail. Which of the choices agrees with the story?

6. This question asks you to choose a statement about the entire story. Don't select an idea that fits only one small part. Your answer should fit all of the story.

7. On the basis of the story, which of the choices is most likely to be true? The answer is not in the story. You will have to think about the ideas and draw your own conclusions.

8. Question 8 asks why. You must select the best explanation from those listed. The cause should be the one given in the article.

9. Question 9 asks you to think about the article ideas in relation to the concept for the group of articles. The statement you select must be true for the article. It should also be a good illustration of the concept in action.

E. Check your work. The answers for the first test are given below. Your teacher may let you use the answer key for other tests. She or he may check your work for you.

F. Put the number correct at the top of your paper. Now go back and recheck the answers that were wrong. Do you see now how the correct answer was better? How can you get ready to do the next test better?

G. Turn to page 186. The directions tell you how to put your score onto a record chart. Your teacher will tell you if you may write in the book. If not, he or she will help you make a copy for your notebook.

Looking for the Big Idea

The next page asks questions about the big ideas in this book. Read the page and think about the ideas.

Just for Fun

Your book has three longer stories that are just for fun. These stories, beginning on pages 54, 98, and 142, are from old folktales. There are no questions to answer.

Answers for Practice Test, page 15		
1. c	2. hemisphere	3. Ann Eckels Bailie
4. a	5. b	6. b
7. a	8. b	9. b

Vocabulary Words and Definitions

PAGE 14

colleagues people a person works with

gravitational like the pull of the force of gravity from inside Earth

hemisphere one-half of a sphere; Earth's northern hemisphere is above the equator, and the southern hemisphere is below the equator

mathematician expert in mathematics

perigee the point where an object in space is closest to Earth

satellite something that orbits a planet in space

PAGE 16

advantage benefit; good luck

antislavery movement in the 19th century to end slavery

editor person who decides what will be published in a magazine

inauguration ceremony making a person president

influenced changed the thinking of someone

journals magazines

Nobel Prize prize given every year to the world's best writers and scientists

publication printing of books and magazines to make them available to the public

publish to print and sell

Pulitzer Prize a prize given every year to American writers

PAGE 18

accurate correct; truthful

astronomer a scientist who studies the planets and the stars

contradicted proved wrong; disagreed with

eventually at a much later time

ridiculed made fun of

scanning looking around

theory idea that hasn't yet been proved

PAGE 20

distortion looking different from the way something really is

effective working correctly; useful

functions works

hinder prevent; get in the way of

Project Mercury an American space mission in the 1960s

turbulence strong movement of air

PAGE 22

bounties rewards of money for doing something

domestic coming from one's own country

erosion the wearing away of soil by wind and water

flourished increased in number; grew and succeeded

Ice Ages the times millions ago when most of Earth was covered with ice

immunity resistance to a disease

myxomatosis (mik sŏ′ mƏ tŏ′ sƏs) a disease that kills rabbits

once-productive useful for growing crops in the past but not now

topsoil the top layer of soil necessary for growing crops

PAGE 24

naturalists people who enjoy nature and the outdoors

overwhelming huge; very important

reclaim to clean up and make healthy again

situated located; built on

PAGE 26

affairs business; things that affect a group

allotment something that is given to people, usually a plot of land

leasing renting; selling the right to something for a period of time

reversed turned around; went back to the old way of doing something

PAGE 28

barriers things that stand in the way

discrimination giving a group different or fewer rights

distinction differences

Hindus a religious group in India

oppressed burdened; not allowed to do some things

PAGE 30

backward nation a nation that is less modern than other nations

communism a political system where the government owns most businesses

serfs people who worked land owned by someone else

toppled caused the end of; tore down

PAGE 32

British Commonwealth former colonies of England that are still connected to it for mutual benefit

domination rule

granted given

PAGE 32 continued
reclaim to get back
reluctant not willing
retained kept; held on to

PAGE 34
drought a time when there is no rain
obscured was in front of; stood in the way
ochre-colored tan; light yellow colored
prospered succeeded; earned money
transformed changed from one thing to another

PAGE 36
expanded got larger; went to more places
expanses large areas of land

PAGE 38
depression hole
elevated raised; built on higher land
temporarily for a short time

PAGE 40
fragments little pieces
site a place where something is or where something happened
submerged under the water
vent a hole at the top of a volcano

PAGE 42
imperial owned by a king or queen
lured pulled toward; tempted
salvage to bring up treasure from sunken ships

PAGE 44
complex complicated; difficult
indirect only partly involved in
mass how much space something takes up
patent proof that someone discovered or invented something
physics the science of matter and energy
uranium a metal that is a source of energy

PAGE 46
congestion crowds; too much in one place
upsurge increase

PAGE 48
cross-section a picture of something sliced in half
diagnosis identifying a disease
graphics pictures
images pictures on a screen
manipulate to move around or change

PAGE 48 continued
tumor something growing in the body

PAGE 50
hobbyists people who do something for fun
ornamental pretty but not useful
primitive early peoples who lived thousands of years ago

PAGE 52
concept idea
detractors people who do not like what you do; critics
impermanence existing for only a short time
installation erection; building
monumental proportions very, very big
parliament a government group that makes the laws
Reichstag (riks´ täk) the German parliament building, where laws were made

PAGES 54–56
gingerly carefully
perch a seat on top of something
referred thought about
tinkered played with
unbolted took apart
whirring noise made by a machine

PAGE 58
constant happening all the time; never ending
exile not being able to go home
friction disagreement
province an area ruled by another country
resented hated
resettle to go back to live in a place
resistance objection; fighting against
supervision responsibility; direction

PAGE 60
embarking leaving a place
plumed having large feathers
resourceful able to think of new ideas
superior better

PAGE 62
three-dimensional showing all sides of something
transmit to send

PAGE 64
intense very strong
radiation energy and heat

PAGE 66
alternative replacement for; thing used instead of something else
extracted taken out of
fermented changed the ingredients of
multistep made of many parts; complicated
toxic emissions poison gases

PAGE 68
aquatic living in water
bladder a container like a balloon that fills with air and floats
clusters small groups
consume to eat
cultivation keeping under control or within limits
dredges machines that clear away unwanted materials
exposition a show or exhibition
milfoil a kind of plant that grows in water
orchidlike like orchids, large and colorful flowers
purification cleanup
vegetation plants

PAGE 70
archeologist a scientist who studies the remains of people
crude basic; simple; not modern
extinct no longer living
fossil the buried remains of an animal that died long ago
paleontologist a scientist who studies how people lived long ago
prehistoric long ago, before people invented language
unearthed dug up

PAGE 72
epidemic a disease that kills most or all of a group
infectious disease that is passed from one person to another; catching
inhabitants people who live in an area
nomadic traveling around without a permanent home

PAGE 74
adjacent next to
capitalist like our economic system, where business operates freely
devised thought up
era age; time
maintained insisted; argued
transition change from one system to another
valid legal

PAGE 76
procedures ways of doing business
transactions the buying and selling of stock
undergo experience; suffer from

PAGE 78
relatively small compared to others; less than
residents the people who live in a place
spewed shot up into the air
testament reminder; honor
vineyard a place where grapes are grown

PAGE 80
generation the time between the birth of someone and the birth of his or her child, about 20 years
mortar material that holds bricks together in buildings
periodic now and then; happening regularly
seeped moved slowly drop by drop
Tenochtitlan the most important city in the Aztec Empire

PAGE 82
crystals small, solid pieces
dissipate to break up and spread out
laser a strong beam of light
mobile able to move around
pulse a beat; burst of energy
sensor a machine that recognizes heat or light
suspended hanging
tension a tightness

PAGE 84
estimate to guess
existed were actually there
scour to dig out
sediment dirt that settles on the ocean bottom
transatlantic crossing the Atlantic Ocean
turbidity muddy and moving quickly

PAGE 86
aluminum a lightweight metal that is easy to bend
conduct to allow electricity to pass through
enable to make possible
gigahertz the measure of very fast speed
silicon a nonmetal element used in computers
vital necessary

PAGE 88
apartheid (∂ pär´ tāt) racial segregation in South Africa
deposits amounts

PAGE 88 continued
enforcing making sure that something happens

PAGE 90
adapted changed something so that it is useful in another way
ammonia a chemical used in fertilizers
blockade to close down; to stand in the way
hydrogen a gas that, with oxygen, makes up water
ingredient a part of something
nitrogen compounds mixtures that contain the gas nitrogen and other things
World War I the war in Europe from 1914 to 1918

PAGE 92
extremes highest and lowest points
pulley a wheel with a rope attached, used to pull heavy weights
resistant not harmed by
sulfur a yellow-colored element often mixed with rubber
vulcanization mixing rubber with sulfur to create a material that does not melt

PAGE 94
dwindling getting smaller
express to show or illustrate
parka-clad wearing a warm jacket with a hood
portrays shows or illustrates
soapstone a kind of stone that is soft enough to carve easily

PAGE 96
confined not allowed to leave a place
crescent shaped like a half circle
intricate complicated and artistic
silversmithing making jewelry and other things out of silver
wavy not straight

PAGES 98–100
bamboo a plant with long hollow stems that mostly grows in China
delicate small and perfect
distressed upset; unhappy
dwell to live in
glimpse a quick look
precious very valuable
willow a beautiful tree with flowing branches and leaves

PAGE 102
access nearness to; ability to use
consult to read
microfilmed photographed in a very small size
network groups that work together

PAGE 104
arthritis a disease that causes pain in the joints of the body
contributions additions to our knowledge
capital the seat of government in a state or country
multimillion more than one million
publishers companies that make books

PAGE 106
analyze to study carefully
anxiety fear and nervousness
competence ability to succeed
innumeracy difficulty understanding mathematics
psychological in the mind; not physical

PAGE 108
artificial satellite a humanmade spacecraft that orbits a planet
Cold War the competition without fighting or armies between the United States and the Soviet Union; the opposite of a "hot" war where people are killed
components individual parts
proposed suggested
unmanned probes spacecraft that do not have astronauts on board

PAGE 110
hatcheries places where baby fish are kept
hydroelectric electricity caused by water power
locales areas; places; locations
replenish to replace what has been lost
spawn give birth to babies
stepped pools a series of pools at different heights
turbines engines

PAGE 112
acid rain rain that mixes with chemicals in the air and becomes polluted
agents things that cause a reaction
devices equipment
disposal getting rid of
Environmental Protection Agency the government group that makes laws to protect the land, air, and water

PAGE 112 continued
ozone the part of the air that protects people from the harmful effects of sunlight
purify to clean; remove poisons from
respiratory having to do with breathing

PAGE 114
anthropologist a scientist who studies people
consequences results
documentation the written record of one's observations
emerging becoming modern; coming out of
evolve to change and grow
mere small; unimportant
sacred relic something old and valuable, usually part of religious beliefs
unindustrialized not using modern tools and machines

PAGE 116
corresponded were equal to
delegates people representing their governments
dialects different forms of a language

PAGE 118
contour planting making farmland high and low rather than flat
densely crowded
depleted made weak and not good for growing crops
illiteracy inability to read and write
urban having to do with cities

PAGE 120
corruption dishonesty
dissolution end; breakup
inflation a rise in prices
unified combined; the same for everyone
World War II the war in Europe from 1939 to 1945

PAGE 122
aerial from the sky

PAGE 124
association a group of people working together
pulpwood wood used to make paper
synthetics humanmade fabrics
woodlots small areas for growing trees

PAGE 126
agency a part of government that has a special job to do
restored brought back

PAGE 126 continued
sources causes; ways to make money
tributaries small streams that feed into larger rivers
widespread extensive; happening to many people

PAGE 128
disastrous causing a lot of damage
excess extra
levee built-up land near a river to prevent flooding
permanently forever
reinforced made stronger

PAGE 130
alloy combination of metals
gyroscope a wheel that spins on an axis to keep a spacecraft steady
iridium a metal
platinum a metal
precision doing something carefully and exactly
vacuum a place without air

PAGE 132
actuaries scientists who study how long people live
insured a person whose family will receive money when he or she dies
life-span how long a person is expected to live
probability what is likely to happen, based on past experience
statistics numbers

PAGE 134
boring cutting holes
chalk bedrock a layer of rock just under the soil, made of chalk
civil engineering building roads and bridges
shuttle train a train that goes back and forth between two places

PAGE 136
automotive engineers people who study how cars can be made better
concentrated paid careful attention to
toll the number of people dead or injured

PAGE 138
humidity moisture in the air
precautions methods to prevent harm
priceless one of a kind; too valuable to put a price on
skylights windows in the ceiling

PAGE 138 continued
ultraviolet a kind of light from the sun that is harmful

PAGE 140
architects people who design buildings
architectural containing architects
bandshell a round building with one open side in which bands and orchestras play music
dingy dark
inadequate too small; not good enough
philharmonic orchestra a very large orchestra
plazas open spaces in a city
rat-infested full of rats
unified similar; belonging together

PAGES 142–144
accord with its own energy; all by itself
acreage farmland
affair concern
bethought remembered; pretended in his mind
brocade heavy cloth with designs on it
colleen an Irish girl
craftily slyly; cleverly
elegant beautiful and expensive
guineas (ghin' ēz) amounts of money in Ireland and England
meandered turned one way and the other
mortal a living person
mused thought about
obliging agreeable
palaver meaningless talk
scabbard a leather holder for a sword
shay a carriage; wagon
sheathed covered by; hidden in
shillelagh (shil ā' le) a short, heavy stick in Ireland
sorcerer a magician
wager a bet
wretched very bad

PAGE 146
constructive useful; practical
demonstrations displays of one's beliefs or desires
dependent caused by; a result of
devote to spend most of your time doing something
ignorance not being educated
instability changing all the time

PAGE 148
heritage something that belongs to all people at all times

PAGE 148 continued
minerals things produced by nature that are not animal or vegetable
nautical on the sea
ratify to agree to make something law
sponsored organized; was in charge of

PAGE 150
composition what something is made of
dense atmosphere full of many gases
turbulence wild movement
unhindered with nothing in the way
vantage point a good place from which to look at something

PAGE 152
dubbed gave a nickname to
efficient good at what they do
thrust a strong push
wedge a shape that is thick at one end and thin at the other end

PAGE 154
cephalothin medicine made from a fungus, a kind of plant
diabetes a disease in which the pancreas, an organ of the body, doesn't work
fungus a plant that is not green, such as mushrooms; *fungi* is the plural of *fungus*
paralysis not being able to move
penicillin a medicine that kills many germs
protein-rich full of things that are good for you
spastic twitching
substances ingredients
ulcers sores in the stomach
yield to contain and give

PAGE 156
breeding reproducing; making plant "babies"
characteristic usually expected
crossbred combined one kind of tree with another kind
cuttings small pieces of trees cut off and planted to make new trees
genetic special features of something: size of leaves or color of flowers
hybrid a new plant made from two different kinds of parent plants

PAGE 156 continued

icon a symbol for something; a cross is often an icon for a religion

immune cannot catch a disease

originated began; came from

resistant usually does not catch a disease

reviving bringing back to life

PAGE 158

adventurous brave; eager to have new experiences

bilingual able to speak two languages

casually easily; without a lot of planning

dominant most important

provincial old-fashioned

regional from only one place

time-consuming taking many hours

trilingual able to speak three languages

PAGE 160

molecules very tiny parts of something

nutrition eating foods that are good for you

reduction making smaller

traits features, such as how tall you are and what color eyes you have

PAGE 162

credit money that is yours to spend

virtually almost

PAGE 164

automation using machines to do people's work

counselor someone who gives advice and help

vending machines machines that sell things like candy and drinks

PAGE 166

dehydrated with all the water taken out

hydroponics growing plants in water instead of in soil

modified changed

nutrient something in food that makes it healthy to eat

PAGE 168

croplands lands where vegetables grow; farms

PAGE 170

molten boiling hot liquid

unfounded not true

PAGE 172

geologists scientists who study Earth

mineral rights permission to use rocks and other things found in an area

PAGE 174

framework rules or way of doing something

opponent the person playing against you

strategies clever ideas

PAGE 176

according to the way it was said; the words Einstein used

billionths tiny pieces of something that is divided into 1,000 million parts

breadth how wide something is; the width

dimension a measure, such as how long, wide, or tall something is

hundredth small pieces of something that is divided into 100 parts

PAGE 178

suburbs country areas right next to cities

thoroughfares streets and roads

PAGE 180

Clean Air Act a law to stop people from polluting the air

emissions smoke and gases

hoppers big boxes

landfill a place that is filled with garbage and then covered with dirt

millennium 1,000 years

monitored watched closely

municipal city

toxic fumes poison gases

PAGE 182

viewer a person who looks at something

PAGE 184

controversy an argument; disagreement

critics people who comment about something

filters materials that change sound

pitch how high or low a sound is

traditional usual; the way something has been in the past

unique very special; not like anything else

I

Change May Produce Unexpected Results

In this section, you will read about surprising effects from certain changes. You will read about these things in the areas of history, biology, anthropology, economics, geography, Earth science, mathematics, engineering, and art.

Keep these questions in mind when you are reading.

1. Do you always get the result that you have worked for?

2. What are some things that have happened that were not intended?

3. Were these unexpected results always good for people?

4. What should be our attitude toward unexpected results?

5. What can be done with unexpected findings?

Look on pages 6-7 for help with words you don't understand in this section.

Shaped Like a Pear

Sailors long ago were often afraid that if they sailed too far from home they would fall off the edge of the flat ocean. In the past, many people had to trust the word of others, for they had no way to gather information for themselves.

Today, we can fly in airplanes high over the earth and see the curve that is proof of its roundness. Astronauts soaring miles high can send us pictures that support our beliefs. Most people now accept the fact that the earth is definitely not flat. But many of them don't realize that it's not exactly round either. Actually, some scientists in the 1950s discovered that the earth is shaped more like a pear, thicker on one end than the other.

A mathematician, Ann Eckels Bailie, used computers to gather information to use in planning space flights. In her work, she figured the distance of spacecraft from the planets and stars.

During her regular work of tracking the second U.S. satellite, Vanguard I, she discovered some facts that didn't seem to make sense. It appeared that the perigee—or point nearest to the earth—of the Vanguard orbit measured a different distance from the northern hemisphere of our earth than from the southern hemisphere.

At first, she and her colleagues thought that the strange figures were due to some mathematical error. But Bailie wouldn't give up the idea that important new information had been discovered. She and the other scientists discussed the shape of the earth again and again. One person even used Silly Putty to show how the earth bulged a little at the equator. Suddenly, Bailie and the others began to see that the same kind of gravitational pull that made the middle bulge might explain the different measurements for the northern and southern hemispheres.

Further research finally supported these beliefs. Bailie's accidental finding gave us a surprising new picture of the shape of the earth.

1. Sailors long ago thought the ocean was
   a. a pear.   c. flat.
   b. round.   d. high.

2. The word in paragraph 5 that means *half of the earth* is _____.

3. The words "a mathematician" in paragraph 3 describe

   _____.

4. While it is not directly stated, the article suggests that
   a. people change their ideas slowly.
   b. more airplanes are needed in science.
   c. people love to change their minds.

5. The perigee is that point in an orbit that is nearest the
   a. satellite.
   b. earth.
   c. computer.

6. On the whole, the article tells about
   a. how most mathematicians work.
   b. an accidental discovery about the earth's shape.
   c. how to track an orbit.

7. Which statement does this article lead you to believe?
   a. Small discoveries can lead to big changes in thought.
   b. Small discoveries aren't worth checking.
   c. Computers aren't much use anymore.

8. Why did Ann Eckels Bailie use computers?
   a. To prove the earth was round.
   b. To gather information for planning space flights.
   c. Because all spacecraft had to carry computers.

9. Think about the concept for this article. Which statement seems true both for the article and for the concept?
   a. Scientists like space study more than mathematics.
   b. New facts can bring about changes in our beliefs.
   c. New facts don't really change old ideas.

Having Their Say

In 1833, Lydia Maria Child put into writing her thoughts about slavery. Her book had a long title: *An Appeal in Favor of the Class of Americans called Africans.* Child knew she was taking a chance, but she didn't expect the angry response she received.

Her friends didn't approve; many people stopped talking to her. She had begun to publish *Juvenile Miscellany,* the first magazine for children, but she had to stop publication because so many people had stopped buying the magazine in protest.

Other unexpected things happened, though, that turned out to be good. Some people started thinking about her words. Others decided to free their slaves after reading her words. Famous writers of the time wrote about her bravery in speaking out.

Lydia Maria Child continued to write and publish antislavery journals. She became the editor for an antislavery journal in New York called *The Standard.* Through this journal, she influenced many thinkers of the times.

Throughout the 1900s, African Americans took advantage of the printed word to put forth their own points of view. One of America's greatest poets was Langston Hughes, an African American who wrote during the first half of the twentieth century. His work is still popular with children as well as adults. But Hughes was no exception. The novelist Toni Morrison won a Pulitzer Prize in 1988 and the Nobel Prize for literature in 1993. Plays written by August Wilson have been awarded two Pulitzer Prizes. The poet Maya Angelou read one of her poems at President Clinton's first inauguration in 1993.

Today the influence of African-American writers extends far beyond the African-American community.

1. Lydia Maria Child published the first
   a. slave book.
   b. want ads.
   c. African book.
   d. children's magazine.

2. The word in paragraph 4 that means *had an effect on* is _____.

3. The words "no exception" in paragraph 5 refer to _____.

4. While it is not directly stated, the article suggests that
   a. people can stop a business by not supporting it.
   b. people need to learn more about writing.
   c. African Americans are better poets than novelists.

5. Some people thought Lydia Maria Child was too
   a. bold.
   b. young.
   c. tired.

6. On the whole, the article tells about
   a. the way children learn to write.
   b. how to start a publishing business.
   c. the power of the printed word to produce change.

7. Which statement does this article lead you to believe?
   a. People don't pay much attention to newspapers.
   b. Writers can influence the way we think.
   c. Writers want to win prizes.

8. Why do African-American writers want to publish their own writings?
   a. Congress passed a law for writers.
   b. They can't get any other jobs.
   c. They want to express their own points of view.

9. Think about the concept for this group of articles. Which statement seems true both for the article and for the concept?
   a. Sticking to an idea may have surprising results.
   b. People should quit if their ideas don't work.
   c. Young people are the best writers of new ideas.

Four Clues from Jupiter

In A.D. 150, the Greek astronomer Ptolemy stated that the sun, moon, planets, and stars all orbited Earth, which stood still. For about 1,300 years, people accepted Ptolemy's theory. Then, a Polish astronomer named Copernicus said that the sun, not Earth, was the center of the solar system. Almost everyone ridiculed Copernicus at that time.

In 1608, shortly after the telescope was invented, the Italian mathematician Galileo built a powerful telescope for his own use. What miracles he saw when he turned his instrument toward the night sky! For the first time, he saw the moon's craters, mountains, and plains. Scanning the vast sky, he saw thousands of stars no one had ever glimpsed before. Then Galileo observed something that contradicted Ptolemy's entire theory about the solar system.

On a cold January night in 1610, Galileo aimed his telescope at the planet Jupiter. He noticed three little stars near the red planet. When he looked the next night, the little stars had changed position. Then, a fourth star appeared. After that, Galileo kept accurate records of the changing positions of the four stars.

Galileo eventually realized that the "little stars" were not stars at all, but satellites in orbit around Jupiter. He decided then that Earth's moon must be orbiting Earth just as Jupiter's satellites orbited Jupiter. Then he began to believe that all the planets, with their orbiting satellites, were in orbit around the sun. Copernicus had been right, after all.

Galileo was soon in trouble with his church and other leaders of European thought. He had to stand trial for teaching false beliefs, and he was placed under house arrest. But his careful records of the little stars' changing positions around Jupiter had unexpectedly confirmed Copernicus' theory and helped correct people's ideas about the solar system.

1. Galileo was an Italian
   - a. mathematician.
   - b. pediatrician.
   - c. optician.
   - d. magician.

2. The word in paragraph 1 that means *made fun of* is _____.

3. The words "no one had ever glimpsed before" in paragraph 2 refer to the thousands of _____.

4. While it is not directly stated, the article suggests that
   - a. Galileo was a fine astronomer.
   - b. the Greek astronomer was right.
   - c. Copernicus was a Spanish writer.

5. Galileo aimed his telescope at the planet
   - a. Jupiter.
   - b. Mercury.
   - c. Venus.

6. On the whole, the article tells about
   - a. keeping accurate records in space.
   - b. Galileo's important discovery.
   - c. satellites that orbit the moon.

7. Which statement does this article lead you to believe?
   - a. No planet can have more than four satellites.
   - b. Galileo was the discoverer of Jupiter's satellites.
   - c. Jupiter orbits its four satellites.

8. Why did Galileo have to stand trial?
   - a. He was accused of fighting with Copernicus.
   - b. He was accused of keeping accurate records.
   - c. He was accused of teaching false beliefs.

9. Think about the concept for this group of articles. Which statement seems true both for the article and for the concept?
   - a. One person's curiosity changed the thinking of 1500 years.
   - b. One person cannot contradict a theory accepted for centuries.
   - c. People should never question statements by ancient scientists.

Seeing from Space

The astronauts who flew around the earth as a part of Project Mercury were explorers entering a new world. Their reports added to our knowledge of how the human body functions outside the earth's gravity. Some of the other things the astronauts reported were very surprising.

For example, scientists were astonished to learn how clearly the astronauts could see things on earth from 100 miles away.

"I saw several houses with smoke coming from the chimneys in the high country around the Himalayas," Gordon Cooper reported after the *Mercury-Atlas* 9 flight of May 1963. Cooper reported seeing a train and the wake of a boat. He also thought he saw a truck moving along a highway.

Photographs were taken from Cooper's capsule. They were clearer than photos taken from high-flying airplanes. This may have been due to the astronaut's cameras being so far away from the air turbulence and dust that cause distortion in photos taken from high-flying airplanes.

Scientists set up vision tests for later astronauts. Certain patterns of white markers were placed on the ground in Texas and Australia. The patterns were kept secret from the astronauts. Yet they easily located the markers and correctly described the patterns.

Today, some scientists think that the earth's gravity may hinder the working of the human eye. For example, on earth gravity may be pulling the soft lens of our eyes out of shape. When the pull of gravity is absent, the soft lens may take on a better shape for seeing clearly. The natural movements of the eye, which help it to see more clearly, may be more effective when a person is "weightless." Whatever the reasons may be for seeing better in space, we are learning new and surprising facts about human vision. The new knowledge is an unplanned result of the space exploration program.

1. Astronauts could see things on earth from
   a. 100 miles away.
   b. high-flying planes.
   c. the Himalayas.
   d. trains and boats.

2. The word in paragraph 4 that means *roughness* or *violence* in the air is

   _____ .

3. The words "with smoke coming from the chimneys" in paragraph 3 describe

   several _____ .

4. While it is not directly stated, the article suggests that
   a. people may learn many surprising things about themselves in space.
   b. space exploration cannot change our knowledge of ourselves.
   c. astronauts have better vision than any other human beings.

5. Certain patterns of white markers were placed on the ground in
   a. Trenton and Alaska.
   b. Tampa and Austria.
   c. Texas and Australia.

6. On the whole, the article tells about
   a. the working of the human eye in space.
   b. natural flickering movements of eyes.
   c. markers and patterns placed on the ground.

7. Which statement does this article lead you to believe?
   a. People are learning new things about the effects of gravity.
   b. Our eyes hurt because gravity is pulling them out of shape.
   c. It is not natural for astronauts to have eyes with soft lenses.

8. Why do we think that the photos were clearer from the capsule than high-flying planes?
   a. Astronauts were given much more expensive cameras.
   b. Air turbulence and dust caused distortion in photos taken in planes.
   c. Cameras do not shake as much in capsules as they do in high planes.

9. Think about the concept for this group of articles. Which statement seems true both for the article and for the concept?
   a. New knowledge is not always the result of planning.
   b. Space experts know everything about man in space.
   c. Earth's gravity only hinders the astronauts.

The Rabbit Invasion

In most parts of the world, rabbits have long been valued for their meat and pelts. Europe has had wild rabbits since the Ice Ages. During the twelfth century, Norman invaders brought European rabbits to England, where the rabbits flourished.

Australia had no rabbits until 1859. Then, an Australian landowner had twenty-four European rabbits sent to him from England. The rabbits multiplied. Four years later, the landowner said that he had killed about 20,000 of them for their meat and pelts. By 1930, the remaining rabbits had multiplied so fast that millions of them had spread over most of Australia.

The rabbits fed on the same grass that nourished Australia's domestic sheep and cattle. The bunnies ate the roots of the grass and chewed off almost every other growing plant they could reach. There was a sharp drop in the number of sheep that an acre of grazing land could feed.

One result of the rabbit invasion was a serious slump in the production of wool, Australia's leading export. And since the rabbit invasion had left the land almost bare of plants, nothing was left to hold down the fertile topsoil. Erosion by wind or water scattered the topsoil and changed once-productive land into useless, desert-like areas.

To solve its rabbit problem, Australia tried bounties, guns, fences, traps, poisons, cats, dogs, and foxes. But it has been myxomatosis (mik sō′ mə tō′ səs), a rabbit disease spread by mosquitoes and rabbit fleas, that finally killed most rabbits. In 1950, the disease killed over 90 percent of Australia's rabbits. Three years later, many of the remaining rabbits had developed an immunity to myxomatosis. Today, Australia's rabbits are still a serious problem.

Although rabbit pelts bring Australia millions of dollars yearly, the money gained is only a small part of the money lost in wool, cattle, and farm crops.

1. Europe has had wild rabbits since the
   a. Rainy Days.
   c. Stone Age.
   b. Ice Ages.
   d. Bronze Age.

2. The word in paragraph 5 that means *a resistance to a disease* is

   _____ .

3. The words "into useless, desert-like areas" in paragraph 4 describe the

   once-productive _____ .

4. While it is not directly stated, the article suggests that
   a. certain animals can destroy the land.
   b. rabbits have been good for Australia.
   c. wool is produced from the fur of rabbits.

5. Myxomatosis is a rabbit disease spread by
   a. cats, dogs, and sheep.
   b. mosquitoes and fleas.
   c. poisons.

6. On the whole, the article tells about
   a. Norman invaders who sent rabbits to Australia.
   b. the effect of the rabbit invasion on Australia.
   c. changing desert lands into productive topsoil.

7. Which statement does this article lead you to believe?
   a. Australia's rabbits are no longer a serious problem these days.
   b. Australia's economy has been affected by the rabbit invasion.
   c. Australia doesn't need money from wool, cattle, or farm crops.

8. Why doesn't myxomatosis still kill Australian rabbits?
   a. Many rabbits have developed an immunity to it.
   b. Myxomatosis only works on cats, dogs, and foxes.
   c. Australians want to keep the rabbits alive.

9. Think about the concept for this group of articles. Which statement seems true both for the article and for the concept?
   a. There was a sharp drop in wool because the rabbits ate the sheep.
   b. Millions of rabbits spread over most of Asia and Africa in 1950.
   c. The rabbit invasion was not foreseen by the Australian landowner.

Don't Tell Her It Can't Be Done

For over a century, the Nashua River in Massachusetts provided power for mills, which gave jobs to thousands of people. Over the years, these paper, cotton, wood, and woolen mills had dumped their waste into its waters.

By the 1960s, the Nashua River was about as polluted as any river could get. Its waters ran red or green or blue with dye from paper mills situated on its banks. The fumes from this dye blackened paint on buildings near the river. In fact, the Nashua River was so polluted that sewage could no longer be dumped into it.

Then along came Marion Stoddart with a simple but overwhelming idea—clean up the Nashua. This was no one-woman campaign. Stoddart was smart and well-organized. She encouraged the paper mills and the business community to form partnerships to reclaim the river. She carried jars of dirty river water to local officials to demonstrate the seriousness of the problem. Stoddart talked with business leaders about economic problems. She talked with environmentalists about the long-term problems of pollution.

Stoddart knew that the Massachusetts state water-pollution-control board would have the final say on forcing the cleanup. When she spoke to the board, she insisted that the Nashua should be made safe for swimming. Many people thought her goals were unrealistic. But she never gave up.

The partnerships Stoddart had helped form and the volunteers who were drawn to her cause never gave up, either. They all realized that cleaning up the river was in everyone's best interests. By 1993, several water treatment plants had been built, and a conservation area called a "greenway" had been created along the banks of the river.

Today mills are still operating along the river, but there are also fish in the river. The Nashua River welcomes boaters, naturalists, and—yes—even swimmers. None of this would have been possible without a woman of vision and a community working together.

1. The Nashua River provided power for
    a. river boats.
    b. mills.
    c. Stoddart's campaign.
    d. the greenway.

2. The word in paragraph 2 that means *located* is _____.

3. The words "conservation area" in paragraph 5 describe _____.

4. While it is not directly stated, the article suggests that
    a. people liked the beautiful red, green, and blue colors of the river.
    b. Marion Stoddart is a conservationist.
    c. paper mill dye and sewage don't mix.

5. Marion Stoddart proved how polluted the river was by
    a. talking with business and political leaders.
    b. swimming in the river.
    c. giving jars of dirty river water to local officials.

6. On the whole, the article tells about
    a. the cooperation necessary to clean up a river.
    b. the difficulties in running a paper mill.
    c. the importance of learning to swim.

7. Which statement does this article lead you to believe?
    a. Nothing ever changes in nature.
    b. Industry, which provides jobs, can also create problems.
    c. Most rivers are as polluted as the Nashua River.

8. Why must individuals, businesses, and government work together to clean up polluted rivers?
    a. The law requires them to work together.
    b. It takes a lot of people to run a mill.
    c. The problem is too big for any one person or group to solve.

9. Think about the concept for this group of articles. Which statement seems true both for the article and for the concept?
    a. Fighting pollution is a losing battle.
    b. One person's determination can create surprising results.
    c. Paper mills are to blame for most of the pollution in Massachusetts.

Failure to Understand

The General Allotment Act, passed in 1887 by the United States Congress, was expected to help Native Americans. The Act called for breaking up tribal reservations and turning them into family-sized farms. Each farm would be given to an individual Native American.

The government thought that Native Americans would be better off if they forgot their tribal organizations and their tribal languages. The government expected Native Americans who owned land and farmed for a living to become more like other Americans.

But it didn't work out that way. The Native Americans were used to living in tribal groups and sharing with each other. They had always thought of land as something that belonged to the whole tribe, rather than to individuals.

With their families scattered on separate farms, many Native Americans were dissatisfied. The land they were given was often poor, and they hadn't the skill to farm it well. Poverty and poor health increased, while the Native Americans clung to their old languages and customs. Eventually the government realized that the division of reservation land had made things worse rather than better for Native Americans.

The Indian Reorganization Act, passed in 1934, reversed the government's policy. This Act said that all Native American land should be owned by tribes, rather than by individuals. The new Act encouraged tribal organizations to take responsibility for running tribal affairs. The Act also provided money, which tribes could borrow to buy more land or to start businesses.

Economic conditions have improved for Native Americans. Many tribes run successful manufacturing, mineral leasing, ranching, hotels, and gambling businesses. Yet problems of unemployment and poor health still exist.

Today Native Americans face a double challenge. They must continue to improve their economic and political position, while at the same time preserving their lands and cultural heritage.

FIND THE ANSWERS

1. The General Allotment Act was expected to help the American
    a. Mexicans.
    b. Indians.
    c. Southerners.
    d. Spaniards.

2. The word in paragraph 4 that means *held fast* is _____.

3. The words "something that belonged to the whole tribe" in paragraph 3 describe the _____.

4. While it is not directly stated, the article suggests that
    a. Most people who own land and farm it are Native Americans.
    b. Native Americans were used to living on ranches.
    c. the government did not understand Native American ways.

5. The government's policy was reversed by the
    a. Indian Reconstruction Bill.
    b. Indian Reorganization Act.
    c. Indian Allotment Program.

6. On the whole, the article tells about
    a. the good land that was given to Native Americans.
    b. an effort to help that didn't work out.
    c. helping Native Americans on their reservations.

7. Which statement does this article lead you to believe?
    a. The government wanted to break up family farms.
    b. Old customs often influence modern life.
    c. New customs are always better than old ones.

8. Why did the government want Native Americans to own land and farm for a living?
    a. It thought this would make the Indians more like other Americans.
    b. It wanted to see if individual Native Americans would drop out of school.
    c. It wanted to see if matters could become worse on the reservation.

9. Think about the concept for this group of articles. Which statement seems true both for the article and for the concept?
    a. A planned change may not always produce the expected results.
    b. The government encouraged Native Americans to drop responsibility.
    c. Economic conditions improved on tribal reservations.

Democracy Comes to India

For centuries, social barriers and religious laws have separated the Hindus of India into class groups called castes. Each caste did only certain work and lived in a certain way. Each caste avoided contact with lower castes.

The Brahmins made up the highest caste. They were priests and scholars who were forbidden to work with their hands. Below them, like rungs on a ladder, were soldiers, merchants, farmers, and laborers.

So low as to be completely outside the caste system were the Untouchables. These people could not live inside the villages, drink water from public wells, or walk on public roads.

In 1947, India became an independent democracy. Three years later, the new government adopted a constitution that did away with discrimination based on caste. Over time, the name Untouchable was changed to *Dalits,* or "oppressed."

The constitution also gave every adult in India the right to vote. Since then, few Brahmins have been elected to high office because they make up such a small caste. The large middle castes and Dalits hold more voting power. In 1997, Kocheril Narayanan became the first of the Dalits to be elected President of India.

Today, many forces are helping to break down the caste barriers. One such force is land reform law. A person may own only a certain amount of land and must use all land owned. As a result, Brahmins are no longer idle landowners collecting rents from large estates. They manage their own small farms; some even plant and harvest crops with their own hands.

The reality of city life is another force that is weakening the caste system. In India, people are moving to the cities to find jobs. Living in crowded apartments, sharing public transportation, and working side by side in factories, forces people from different castes into contact with each other. In India's crowded cities, some caste distinctions are being forgotten.

Unexpectedly, it is the new forces at work in India that are doing more to break down the caste system than the 1950 constitution that made discrimination illegal.

1. The highest castes in India were the
   a. builders.
   b. bankers.
   c. Brahmins.
   d. Burmese.

2. The word in paragraph 6 that means *differences* is _____.

3. The words "living in crowded apartments" in paragraph 6 tell about the different _____.

4. While it is not directly stated, the article suggests that
   a. priests and scholars were untouchable.
   b. the Untouchables led miserable lives.
   c. all Untouchables were rich people.

5. Every adult in India was given the right to vote in
   a. 1509.
   b. 1590.
   c. 1950.

6. On the whole, the article tells about
   a. the caste system in India.
   b. sharing transportation.
   c. drinking from public wells.

7. Which statement does this article lead you to believe?
   a. Brahmins are leaving India to start a caste system here.
   b. The caste system is losing its importance in India.
   c. Every country should have a caste system like India's.

8. Why have very few Brahmins been elected to high office since 1950?
   a. The middle castes and Untouchables hold more voting power.
   b. They do not want to serve in high office in a democracy.
   c. They prefer to spend their time walking on public roads.

9. Think about the concept for this group of articles. Which statement seems true both for the article and for the concept?
   a. The Brahmins were soldiers, merchants, and farmers.
   b. Some social barriers are being broken down by the forces of democracy.
   c. Brahmins and Dalits have always been close friends.

Window to the West

For hundreds of years, Russia was a backward nation because it had no good seaport. Czar Peter the Great, who ruled Russia from 1689 to 1725, fought a war with Sweden to gain seaports on the Baltic Sea. He founded a new Baltic seaport, St. Petersburg, and made it Russia's capital.

Czar Peter's aim was to make Russia a world power by introducing foreign trade. He felt that foreign money could help to develop his country's natural resources and to build up its industry. The new seaport was a "window to the west" that made his plan possible.

When Czar Peter died, Russia was producing more iron than any European country. New factories were busy making supplies for Russia's army. Russia was becoming a world power. But the country was changing in a way that was not part of Czar Peter's plan.

Before Czar Peter's reign, Russia's population was made up of two groups—the serfs who worked on the farms, and the wealthy, landowning nobles. The Czars had complete power over everyone. But now foreign trade and the new industries produced new groups made up of merchants, factory owners, and factory workers. These groups developed interests and demands of their own. Peter and many of the Czars who followed him used their powers ruthlessly to crush all groups that resisted them.

By the late 1800s, most of the Russian people were dissatisfied and angry. The merchants and factory owners were demanding more voice in the government. The serfs, freed in 1861, wanted land, and the factory workers wanted better wages and working conditions.

In 1917, the Russian people revolted. They toppled the hated government of Czar Nicholas II and eventually established communism. By the 1940s Russia had indeed become a world power. But the Russian people did not like communism. In 1991 they rose again and established a government more like that of the United States, with an elected president.

Czar Peter could never have guessed what would happen to Russia when he set out long ago to make his country a world power.

30

1. Russia was a backward nation because it had no good
    a. seaport.   c. windows.
    b. capital.   d. navy.

2. The word in paragraph 4 that means *showing no mercy or pity* is
    _____.

3. The words "a world power" in the last paragraph describe
    _____.

4. While it is not directly stated, the article suggests that
    a. Russia was once mostly an agricultural nation.
    b. serfs owned all the land in Russia long ago.
    c. the wealthy nobles worked the farms themselves.

5. Before Czar Peter's reign, Russia was made up of
    a. merchants and workers.
    b. serfs and nobles.
    c. Czars and Swedes.

6. On the whole, the article tells about
    a. factory workers who wanted better wages.
    b. the changes that have taken place in Russia.
    c. the weak government of Czar Nicholas II.

7. Which statement does this article lead you to believe?
    a. Merchants demanded the Czars have more control over Russia.
    b. The Russian people were always completely satisfied with the Czars.
    c. The Russian people took action when they did not like their government.

8. Why did the Czars use their powers ruthlessly?
    a. They wished to change Russia's population.
    b. They wished to crush all groups resisting them.
    c. They wanted to give factory workers good wages.

9. Think about the concept for this group of articles. Which statement seems true both for the article and for the concept?
    a. Czar Peter the Great ruled Sweden from St. Petersburg.
    b. Czar Peter could not have predicted his far-reaching influence.
    c. St. Petersburg is the only seaport Russia has ever had.

The Price of Victory

One might expect a strong and wealthy nation that wins its wars to become even wealthier and more powerful. Yet Great Britain, which won victories in both world wars, lost most of its overseas empire, much of its wealth, and its position of leadership in the world.

At the beginning of World War I, Great Britain was the richest and strongest nation in the world. The British Navy controlled the seas. The British monarch ruled one-fourth of the world's population. Large amounts of British money were invested throughout the world.

When World War I was over, Great Britain had retained its colonies, but some of them were becoming restless. In Africa and Asia, British colonials had seen their rulers fighting other Europeans. They had lost some of their respect for Great Britain. To pay for the war, Britain had to reclaim money that had been invested overseas.

World War II also cost Great Britain large sums of money. German bombs had damaged English cities and demolished English factories. Forced to fight on several different fronts, the British armed forces could no longer protect all of Great Britain's distant colonies. The Japanese soon occupied certain Asian colonies.

When World War II was over, more colonies in Asia were reluctant to return to British domination. India and the British colonies in Africa demanded self-rule. Granted their independence, these new nations kept a few bonds with Britain as members of the British Commonwealth, but the empire was no longer a great source of wealth.

Britain could no longer afford a great navy. Instead of lending money to other nations, Britain had to borrow money.

Great Britain won its wars, but the price of victory was unexpectedly high.

FIND THE ANSWERS

1. Some of Great Britain's colonies in Asia were occupied by the
   - a. Portuguese.
   - c. Chinese.
   - b. Vietnamese.
   - d. Japanese.

2. The word in paragraph 2 that means *king or queen* is _____.

3. The words "forced to fight on several different fronts" in paragraph 4 refer to the British _____ _____.

4. While it is not directly stated, the article suggests that
   - a. Great Britain is as strong as ever.
   - b. Great Britain still rules the world.
   - c. Great Britain is now a poor country.

5. India and the British colonies in Africa demanded
   - a. self-rule.
   - b. some bonds.
   - c. more money.

6. On the whole, the article tells about
   - a. damaged English cities and demolished factories.
   - b. the price Great Britain has paid for its wars.
   - c. large amounts of money Britain has invested.

7. Which statement does this article lead you to believe?
   - a. Great Britain became stronger and wealthier.
   - b. Wars are the only way to settle arguments.
   - c. Wars can be costly in many different ways.

8. Why did Great Britain have to reclaim much of its money from overseas?
   - a. Great Britain needed the money to pay for the war.
   - b. Great Britain wanted money to demolish its factories.
   - c. Great Britain needed the money to buy German bombs.

9. Think about the concept for this group of articles. Which statement seems true both for the article and for the concept?
   - a. When World War II was over, Britain was ruled by colonials.
   - b. One result of World War II was the creation of new nations.
   - c. Very few changes are ever brought about by world wars.

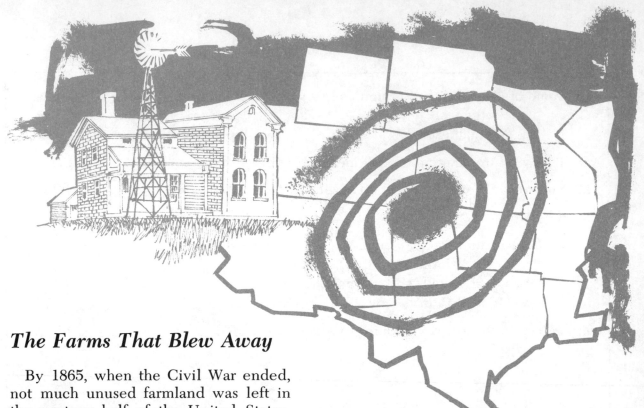

The Farms That Blew Away

By 1865, when the Civil War ended, not much unused farmland was left in the eastern half of the United States. But farther west, on the Great Plains that included the Dakotas and the western parts of Kansas and Nebraska, there was plenty of free land for the taking.

Those who had visited the Great Plains said that the land closely resembled the fertile prairies of Illinois and eastern Kansas. The dark brown soil was thickly blanketed with rich grass. Railroads were being built across the Plains, and settlers would eventually be able to ship farm products from there to eastern markets.

Many settlers migrated west to the Great Plains. They plowed up the deep-rooted wild grasses that had held down the fertile topsoil, and they planted wheat and corn.

The settlers learned, in time, that the Great Plains was not like Illinois or eastern Kansas. For one thing, there was less rainfall; and rainfall varied widely from year to year. Strong winds blew all summer long. In drought years, crops died and the loosened topsoil that was no longer anchored by the roots of the grasses blew away. In good years, when there was better-than-average rainfall, farmers prospered.

Then, in the 1930s, disaster struck. One dry year followed another. Lakes, rivers, and wells went dry. In 1933, people in New York and other eastern cities saw ochre-colored clouds that sometimes obscured the sun. They were dust clouds, and they contained some of the fertile topsoil of the Great Plains.

The settlers who moved to the western plains had not expected to destroy the land they tried to farm. But they nearly transformed it into a desert. They gave to some parts of the Great Plains a new name—the Dust Bowl.

FIND THE ANSWERS

1. The new name given to the Great Plains by the settlers was the
   - a. Sugar Bowl.
   - c. Rose Bowl.
   - b. Dirty Bowl.
   - d. Dust Bowl.

2. The word in paragraph 5 that means *darkened or hid from sight* is

   _____ .

3. The words "that had held down the fertile topsoil" in paragraph 3 describe the

   deep-rooted wild _____ .

4. While it is not directly stated, the article suggests that
   - a. rainfall in the Great Plains is the same all year long.
   - b. the Great Plains might have been saved if used properly.
   - c. it is easy to replace fertile topsoil once it is gone.

5. The Great Plains included the Dakotas and the western parts of
   - a. Kalamazoo and Nome.
   - b. Kansas and Nebraska.
   - c. Kentucky and New York.

6. On the whole, the article tells about
   - a. ochre-colored clouds that were seen in New York.
   - b. the deep-rooted wild grasses in the Dakotas.
   - c. the result of poor farming in the Great Plains.

7. Which statement does this article lead you to believe?
   - a. Crops of wheat and corn grow better in dust than topsoil.
   - b. Many people besides farmers are affected by a crop failure.
   - c. Crops are important only to the people who grow them today.

8. Why did disaster strike in the 1930s?
   - a. Gentle winds blew all winter long.
   - b. There was too much of a rainfall.
   - c. One dry year followed another.

9. Think about the concept for this group of articles. Which statement seems true
   both for the article and for the concept?
   - a. The settlers didn't realize how their farming would affect the land.
   - b. The farmers learned that the Great Plains were like eastern Kansas.
   - c. The farmers prospered when ochre-colored clouds obscured the sun.

Of Time and the Railroads

Those who planned and constructed the first American railroads were people of great vision. They predicted that their "iron horses" would open vast expanses of land to farming and industry. They knew that towns would spring up along the new railroads. Yet few of these pioneers could have guessed that American railroads would establish the system of time used throughout most of the world today.

Until the 1880s, all time in the United States was sun time. Farmers set their clocks to noon when the sun appeared to be overhead. In towns, people set their clocks by a courthouse clock or factory whistles. One town's time was often different from the time in a neighboring town.

As the new railroads expanded, large numbers of people began to travel. But the railroads were unable to print accurate timetables when most towns along their tracks had their clocks set differently. There was need for a change, and the railroads led in planning it.

In 1883, railroads in the United States and Canada adopted standard time, a system that divided the continent into four time zones. Within each zone, all railroad clocks were set to an identical time. When it was noon in the Eastern Zone, it was eleven o'clock in the Central Zone, ten o'clock in the Mountain Zone, and nine o'clock in the Pacific Zone. Railroad time signals were sent out by the newly invented telegraph.

Standard time quickly spread. Traveling business people set their watches to match the railroad clocks. Factories and schools followed the railroad's lead. Soon, nearly everyone in the United States and Canada was using the four-zone time system—standard time.

Today, nearly all the world keeps standard time according to an international system of twenty-four time zones.

1. Until the 1880s, all time in the United States was
    a. fun time.   c. spring time.
    b. sun time.   d. moon time.

2. The word in paragraph 5 that means *agree with* is _____.

3. The words "of great vision" in paragraph 1 describe the _____.

4. While it is not directly stated, the article suggests that
    a. farmers set their clocks according to the factory whistles.
    b. the correct time was not too important before the 1800s.
    c. only people who traveled on trains ever knew the time.

5. Railroad time signals were sent out by the newly invented
    a. television.
    b. telephone.
    c. telegraph.

6. On the whole, the article tells about
    a. pioneers who rode on "iron horses."
    b. large numbers of people who traveled.
    c. the establishment of standard time.

7. Which statement does this article lead you to believe?
    a. Accurate timetelling is important to many industries.
    b. Accurate time is important only in the United States.
    c. Accurate time is owned by the people who built railroads.

8. Why weren't railroads able to print accurate timetables?
    a. Towns along the tracks set their clocks differently.
    b. No one was able to read timetables that were accurate.
    c. Farmers preferred to read the sun instead of timetables.

9. Think about the concept for this group of articles. Which statement seems true both for the article and for the concept?
    a. It is much better to run a railroad on courthouse time.
    b. Railroads in Canada refused to accept a standard time system.
    c. The need for standard time zones was not unexpected by early railroad planners.

When the Mississippi
Flowed Backward

In 1811, a giant earthquake shook the Mississippi Valley. Although the earthquake did not cause great destruction of property or much loss of life, it may have been the most severe earthquake ever felt in North America.

The quake began late in 1811 as a series of shocks that were most violent near New Madrid, Missouri. There were no large cities in that area. The few settlers lived mostly in log cabins, which resist earthquakes better than most types of houses.

John James Audubon, the naturalist and painter, was riding horseback in Kentucky when he felt, and saw, the land rising and falling around him. "The earth waved like a field of corn before the breeze," he said. Other people as far distant as New Orleans, Boston, and Canada felt the shocks.

The giant earthquake had many un-expected results. At one point along the Mississippi River, high banks fell into the river from both sides of the stream. The water was forced to the center of its channel where it rose so high that it flowed upstream temporarily.

Large areas were elevated and left 5 to 20 feet higher than they had been. Other areas sank and became swamps or lakes. In western Tennessee, the earthquake lowered a forest 20 feet. Water filled the depression and formed a lake. The trees died, but some of their stumps are still standing.

Lake Eulalie just disappeared. The earthquake opened up two cracks in the lake floor, and its water drained away. A few years later, trees grew where the lake had been.

All in all, about a million square miles of land was affected by the giant earthquake of December 16, 1811.

FIND THE ANSWERS

1. In western Tennessee, the earthquake lowered a
   a. fountain.
   b. farmer.
   c. forest.
   d. flower.

2. The word in paragraph 5 that means *a hollow or lowered area* is

   _____.

3. The words "which resist earthquakes better than most types of houses" in

   paragraph 2 describe the log _____.

4. While it is not directly stated, the article suggests that
   a. an earthquake makes violent and sudden changes in the land.
   b. earthquakes cannot change the land in any important way.
   c. the shocks of an earthquake are rarely felt at any distance.

5. A giant earthquake shook the Mississippi Valley in
   a. 1999.
   b. 1118.
   c. 1811.

6. On the whole, the article tells about
   a. the effects of a giant earthquake.
   b. a naturalist and painter on a horse.
   c. two cracks in the floor of a lake.

7. Which statement does this article lead you to believe?
   a. The land looked very different before 1811.
   b. The face of the land is always the same.
   c. Lakes cannot disappear and forests cannot die.

8. Why did Lake Eulalie disappear?
   a. The earthquake lowered a large number of trees over it.
   b. Its water drained away through two cracks in the lake floor.
   c. It was covered by about a million square miles of land.

9. Think about the concept for this group of articles. Which statement seems true both for the article and for the concept?
   a. Rivers can never flow upstream, even briefly.
   b. Changes in nature cannot always be predicted.
   c. An earthquake rarely produces unexpected change.

The Now-and-Then Island

The floor of the Pacific Ocean is dotted with volcanoes. Some have erupted so often that they have built up islands of hardened lava. Japan, Hawaii, Guam, and the Aleutians are all islands built by volcanoes.

In 1952 men had a rare opportunity to observe this process of island-building, for in September of that year, scientific instruments on shore indicated that a submerged volcano named Myojin had suddenly become active. A Japanese ship steamed out to investigate Myojin, which lies 250 miles south of Tokyo.

The men on board the ship saw a remarkable sight. Jagged black rocks had formed a new island several hundred feet long. The heat was so great that water around the rocks boiled, while clouds of steam and gas rose high in the air.

A few days later the island disappeared. The cooling rock had formed a plug that sealed the vent of the volcano.

When pressure built up again inside the volcano, new and violent eruptions occurred. The island was torn apart, and the rocks sank beneath the surface of the sea.

A Japanese research ship reached the site on September 24. This ship may have been directly over the volcano when it erupted a third time. A few fragments of the ship were found later. All thirty-one people aboard were lost.

The island appeared once again when new masses of lava were thrown up. For a while, a steep-sided cone of rock rose 300 feet above the sea.

Mapmakers wondered if they should mark Myojin on their charts as an island. Was it there to stay?

A year after the first Japanese ship had visited Myojin, United States ships visited the site, not knowing what to expect. They found only a calm sea. Myojin was quiet again, and the island was gone.

FIND THE ANSWERS

1. Myojin lies 250 miles south of
    a. Tokyo.   c. Toledo.
    b. Toronto.   d. Tampico.

2. The word in paragraph 2 that means *sunk under water* is

    _____ .

3. The words "that sealed the vent of the volcano" in paragraph 4 describe a

    _____ .

4. While it is not directly stated, the article suggests that
        a. rocks in the Pacific Ocean are boiled.
        b. some research work may be dangerous.
        c. Japan erupted from a volcano in 1952.

5. The floor of the Pacific Ocean is dotted with
        a. vultures.
        b. volcanoes.
        c. vampires.

6. On the whole, the article tells about
        a. mapmakers who wonder about their charts.
        b. a Japanese research ship in the Pacific.
        c. an island that appeared and disappeared.

7. Which statement does this article lead you to believe?
        a. The land is still changing.
        b. Only Japanese live on islands.
        c. All volcanoes are submerged.

8. Why were only fragments of the Japanese research ship found?
        a. It may have sailed to another area in the Pacific Ocean.
        b. The Japanese scientists took pieces of the ship home.
        c. It may have been over the volcano when it erupted.

9. Think about the concept for this group of articles. Which statement seems true both for the article and for the concept?
        a. Islands may make an unexpected appearance in an ocean.
        b. Volcanoes that are submerged are no longer very active.
        c. Once an island disappears it can never be expected to appear again.

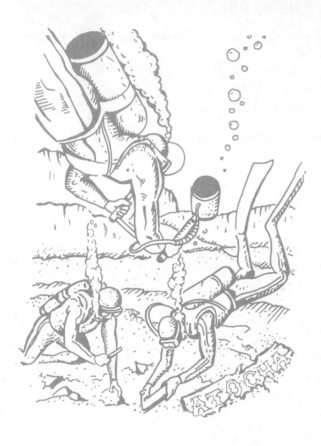

One Word and a World of Difference

Mel Fisher was a scuba diver who became one of the most famous treasure hunters in history. In 1966, stories of Spanish shipwrecks lured Mel to the Florida Keys. According to Spanish records, two imperial Spanish treasure ships—*Nuestra Señora de Atocha* and *Santa Margarita*—sank near the Keys of Matecumbe in a hurricane in 1622. Mel was determined to locate those ships and salvage their treasure. He searched near the islands of Upper and Lower Matecumbe off southern Florida for months with no success.

A friend of Mel's, Eugene Lyon, was studying in Spain. One day in 1970, he happened to find a document dated 1622. The pages were old and worm-eaten. At the end of the document, Lyon read that the *Margarita* sank near the Marquesas Keys. Lyon looked at old maps of the Florida Keys and learned that at the time of the shipwrecks, *all* the Keys were called Matecumbe. The Marquesas Keys referred to in the old document were about a hundred miles from Mel's current location.

As soon as Mel learned this, he moved his salvage ships to the new site. In 1970, Mel received a copy of another document from Spain that said the *Atocha* sank east of the last Key. He searched that area for several months, but found nothing. Meanwhile, the people who had invested their money in the search were becoming restless.

Then Eugene Lyon made an important discovery about the latest documents that Mel had received. He realized that an error had been made in copying the ancient handwriting. The original documents said that the ships sank to the *veste* of the island, not to the *este*. *West*, not *east*! Mel moved his salvage ships again— this time to the west of the Marquesas. And there, in June of 1971, he found the treasure of the *Santa Margarita*.

It took several more years for Mel to locate the *Atocha* and to recover its fortune in gold, silver, and jewels. However, he might still be looking in the wrong place if his friend hadn't noticed that one wrong word.

1. Historical research into old documents can be used to
    a. find the Florida Keys.
    c   find lost treasure.
    b. learn about scuba diving.
    d. study foreign languages.

2. The word in paragraph 1 that means *recover lost property* is
    _____.

3. The word "worm-eaten" in paragraph 2 describes _____.

4. While it is not directly stated, the article suggests that

    a. Mel Fisher and Eugene Lyon met in college.
    b. It takes a lot of money to search for sunken treasure.
    c. Hunting for sunken treasure is a waste of time.

5. Eugene Lyon discovered that
    a. worms eat important documents.
    b. a word had been copied incorrectly.
    c. Mel Fisher was searching in water that was too shallow.

6. On the whole, the article tells about
    a. the time and dedication required of treasure hunters.
    b. the importance of being able to read and speak a foreign language.
    c. the dangers of hurricanes.

7. Which statement does this article lead you to believe?
    a. Mel Fisher refused to share his treasure with Eugene Lyon.
    b. Mel Fisher should have learned Spanish.
    c. Eugene Lyon loved to solve ancient mysteries.

8. Why do treasure hunters refer to ancient documents?
    a. They are hard to read, and treasure hunters like a challenge.
    b. They contain the most accurate eyewitness information available.
    c. They were written by Spaniards.

9. Think about the concept for this group of articles. Which statement seems true both for the article and for the concept?
    a. Scuba diving provides both fun and profit.
    b. Diving for sunken treasure can be dangerous.
    c. A simple mistake can have far-reaching consequences.

The Theory That Exploded

In 1902, no one would hire twenty-three-year-old Albert Einstein as a professor of physics, so he took a job as clerk in a Swiss patent office. In his spare time he concentrated on his own scientific theories.

In 1905, three of Einstein's theories were published. One theory dealt with matter and energy. The theory contained a formula that looked very simple: $E = mc^2$. It means that the energy (E) in any amount of matter equals the mass (m) of the matter (the amount of material in the matter) multiplied by the speed of light squared (c^2). It was a short formula, but Einstein developed it through extremely complex mathematics.

Until Einstein's theory of matter and energy was published, scientists believed that matter and energy were different things. Energy was power, or the ability of a system to do work, while matter was anything you could actually weigh.

Einstein's short formula states that matter and energy are just different forms of the same thing. Matter can change into energy, and energy into matter. Einstein showed scientists how to calculate the amount of energy in a known amount of matter. A pound of matter, said Einstein, contains energy enough to send an ocean liner across the Atlantic and back.

Einstein's theory opened up new questions. How could the energy in matter be unlocked? How would this energy be used? Not until 1942 did scientists find a way to unlock the energy in the uranium atom.

The young Einstein who clerked in the Swiss patent office had not expected that his formula would first be put to use in the atomic bombs exploded over Japan in 1945. Speaking of atomic energy, Dr. Einstein later said, "My part in it was quite indirect. I did not, in fact, foresee that it would be released in my time."

FIND THE ANSWERS

1. Scientists first unlocked energy in the uranium
   - a. bomb.
   - b. light.
   - c. atom.
   - d. cell.

2. The word in paragraph 2 that means *very complicated* or *difficult to understand* is _____ .

3. The words "who clerked in the Swiss patent office" in the last paragraph describe the young _____ .

4. While it is not directly stated, the article suggests that
   - a. scientists knew matter and energy were the same.
   - b. Albert Einstein was a brilliant scientist.
   - c. Einstein's formulas were developed simply.

5. The first atomic bombs were exploded in 1945 over
   - a. Japan.
   - b. China.
   - c. Tibet.

6. On the whole, the article tells about
   - a. scientific theories that are not published.
   - b. Einstein's theory of matter and energy.
   - c. the Swiss patent office and its clerks.

7. Which statement does this article lead you to believe?
   - a. The first atomic bomb was used in a Swiss patent office.
   - b. Einstein knew that atomic energy would be released in his time.
   - c. Einstein didn't want his formula used to make atomic bombs.

8. Why did Einstein take a job as a clerk?
   - a. He thought it would help to see the patents.
   - b. He wanted to work in a shoe store selling shoes.
   - c. No one would hire him as a professor of physics.

9. Think about the concept for this group of articles. Which statement seems true both for the article and for the concept?
   - a. Einstein's theory was completely wrong.
   - b. Einstein's theory was not important.
   - c. Einstein's theory changed our world.

From Planes to Trains?

In 1945, United States railroads carried nearly 900 million passengers. In 1965, they carried a little more than 300 million. During the same twenty years, the number of passengers carried by airlines soared from 7 million to nearly 100 million.

The great upsurge in air travel was largely due to the airplanes developed during and after World War II. Because these new airplanes were larger than prewar planes, they could carry more passengers at lower fares than ever before. And the newer planes were much faster than prewar airliners had been. For example, jet-powered airliners are almost twice as fast as prewar airliners.

But the capacity and speed of the new airliners have created unexpected problems for air travelers. Most jet aircraft require long runways, and some cities have had to relocate their airports far from their downtown areas. As a result, it may take an air traveler a long time to travel to and from an airport.

The increased number of flights scheduled by the airlines has caused air traffic congestion at some large airports. During rush hours, many airlines want to use the same runways at the same time. Some planes have to circle overhead waiting their turns to land. Others must line up on the taxiways waiting their turns to take off.

The United States must solve its air travel problems soon. Otherwise, rail travel may be due for a comeback. Trains are much slower than planes, but they usually depart and arrive on schedule. And they carry their passengers from a downtown station in one city to a downtown station in another city. One of America's largest railroads is already running high-speed passenger trains between New York City and Washington, D.C. In both of these busy cities, airplane traffic jams have caused unexpected delays. The resulting inconvenience affects hundreds of air travelers and the businesses that brought them to the city.

46

FIND THE ANSWERS

1. Most jet aircraft require long
   - a. runways.
   - b. raceways.
   - c. causeways.
   - d. breakaways.

2. The word in paragraph 3 that means *the power or ability to do something* is

   _____ .

3. The words "soared from 7 million to nearly 100 million" in paragraph 1 describe the number of _____ .

4. While it is not directly stated, the article suggests that
   - a. the best way to travel is by steamboat.
   - b. more people may start using trains again.
   - c. there is no congestion in air traffic.

5. The great upsurge in air travel developed during and after
   - a. the Civil War.
   - b. World War II.
   - c. the War of the Roses.

6. On the whole, the article tells about
   - a. New York City and Washington.
   - b. rush hours in our cities.
   - c. problems in air travel.

7. Which statement does this article lead you to believe?
   - a. During rush hours, many airlines build their own runways.
   - b. An airplane always takes off and lands on schedule.
   - c. Passengers are upset by delays in air travel.

8. Why is there congestion at some large airports?
   - a. Trains bring their passengers directly to large airports.
   - b. Airlines have scheduled an increased number of flights.
   - c. Passengers must all take the same plane at the same time.

9. Think about the concept for this group of articles. Which statement seems true both for the article and for the concept?
   - a. Faster means of travel have created slowdowns in some areas.
   - b. Airports are always in the downtown areas of large cities.
   - c. Trains are much faster than planes when they are on schedule.

Seeing by Computer

Have you ever watched a lifelike Tyrannosaurus Rex thunder across a movie screen, or seen cows moo-ving their lips as they tell you what brand of milk to buy? If so, you have seen computer graphics at work.

Computers are being used more and more to create images that entertain, persuade, inspire, or protect us. You may be most familiar with these images, or computer graphics, in movies and advertisements. But computer graphics are also being used routinely in fields such as medicine, art, and engineering.

One use of computer graphics in medicine is the CAT scan, short for *computerized axial tomography*. The CAT scan allows a doctor to see what is going on inside a patient's body. For example, a doctor may order a CAT scan to see if a patient has a brain tumor. First the patient lies flat on a table while the brain is x-rayed from several angles. Then a computer puts the x-ray images together and creates a cross-section of the brain. This helps the doctor to make a diagnosis without having to perform surgery.

Computer graphics are also used in surprising ways by artists to create new forms of beauty. Some artists use the ability of the computer to create images. Other artists draw their own picture on the computer screen and then manipulate that picture by changing its shape, size, color, or position. There was a time when some people felt that computer art wasn't art at all. However, computer art now hangs in art galleries and museums along with other masterpieces.

An engineer who is, for example, designing a bridge will use computer graphics to show how all the pieces of the bridge fit together. Then the engineer can manipulate the computer image to show what will happen to the bridge under certain conditions, such as high winds, heavy traffic, and earthquakes. The engineer can then change the design of the bridge to help it meet those conditions.

What began as a time-saving tool has become a life-saving tool and a life-enhancing tool, as well.

48

1. Computers are being used more and more to create
    - a. brain tumors.
    - b. graphic images.
    - c. art galleries.
    - d. engineers.

2. The word in paragraph 3 that means *determination of disease* is
    _____.

3. The words "high winds, heavy traffic, and earthquakes" in paragraph 5
    describe _____.

4. While it is not directly stated, the article suggests that
    - a. computers encourage people to have CAT scans.
    - b. cows make better salesmen than people.
    - c. we keep inventing new uses for computers.

5. A doctor can use computer graphics to make a
    - a. commercial.
    - b. diagnosis.
    - c. picture.

6. On the whole, the article tells about
    - a. different uses for computer graphics.
    - b. a new form of art.
    - c. how to make a Tyrannosaurus Rex appear lifelike.

7. Which statement does this article lead you to believe?
    - a. One day computers will rule the entire world.
    - b. The computer can act as an extension of the human hand and eye.
    - c. Oil painting is the only true art form.

8. Why do engineers make computer models of bridges?
    - a. They like to watch earthquakes.
    - b. It's fun working with computers.
    - c. They want to make their bridges safer.

9. Think about the concept for this group of articles. Which statement seems
    true both for the article and for the concept?
    - a. Engineers object to having artists use computers.
    - b. A useful tool is making our lives safer and more fun.
    - c. Doctors and engineers are artists because they use computer graphics.

From Campfire to Museum

When clay is heated to a certain temperature, a chemical change takes place. The clay becomes hard and water cannot make it soft again.

It was probably an accident that taught prehistoric people to make pottery by firing objects made of clay. Perhaps a piece of dried clay was dropped into a cooking fire. When the ashes cooled, someone picked up the fragment and saw that the clay had changed. It was much harder, and it no longer grew soft when wet. For the people of ancient times, this discovery was very useful. It allowed them to make vessels for carrying and storing liquids.

Even the earliest pottery was usually decorated in some way. The ancient maker of a water jar may have used a pointed stick to scratch zigzag lines on the clay surface before the jar was fired. Sometimes a seashell or a woven mat was used to press patterns into the soft clay. As early as 3000 B.C., potters were painting designs on their jars. They used different kinds of clay mixed with water to produce different colors.

Primitive potters also fired many clay objects that were purely ornamental. In ancient Egypt, potters made clay jewelry. In Babylonia, potters made colored clay tiles to decorate buildings. In South America, potters made religious statues and musical instruments of clay.

Pottery-making is a useful craft that became an art. Although, most of the bowls, jars, and plates used today are made in factories, the making and firing of pottery by hand continues. It is a popular hobby. Professional artists also work with clay. But many of the beautiful vessels made by hobbyists and professional artists are not used for everyday purposes. Instead, they are displayed as art objects in homes and in art museums and galleries.

50

1. In ancient Egypt, potters made clay
   - a. artists.
   - b. crafts.
   - c. galleries.
   - d. jewelry.

2. The word in paragraph 2 that means *a piece broken off from something* is

   _____ .

3. The words "that were purely ornamental" in paragraph 4 describe the clay

   _____ .

4. While it is not directly stated, the article suggests that
   - a. making pottery is an ancient art.
   - b. pottery is a modern kind of craft.
   - c. only professional artists make pottery.

5. A chemical change takes place in clay when it is
   - a. dropped.
   - b. heated.
   - c. designed.

6. On the whole, the article tells about
   - a. the history of pottery-making.
   - b. ancient Babylonian decorations.
   - c. religious statues in South America.

7. Which statement does this article lead you to believe?
   - a. Clay is an ancient substance no longer used.
   - b. Clay can be molded easily into many shapes.
   - c. Clay is a very difficult material for artists to use.

8. Why is some pottery still made by hand?
   - a. It is a popular hobby.
   - b. Factories insist upon it.
   - c. It is a good way to get rich.

9. Think about the concept for this group of articles. Which statement seems true both for the article and for the concept?
   - a. People long ago were against the use of pottery.
   - b. It is wrong to make use of an accidental discovery.
   - c. Valuable discoveries are sometimes made accidentally.

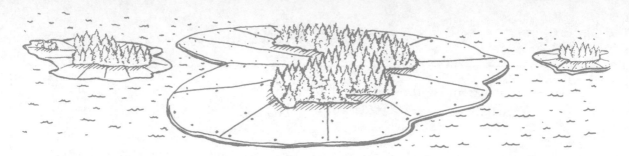

Packaging Art

Artists challenge us to see the world in new and unusual ways. For many people, "art" consists of famous paintings and sculptures. Such masterpieces are exhibited in museums, where they are carefully protected so that they will last as long as possible. Nothing could be further from this concept of art than the works of the artist Christo, who seeks the "special beauty of impermanence."

Christo wraps things of monumental proportions in huge pieces of fabric, invites the public to look at them and take pictures, and then just as quickly removes the wrappings. Some of his earlier wrapping were in remote locations. In 1969, Christo created *Wrapped Coast* by wrapping a mile-long section of the Australian coast to create a new cliff. In 1976, he created *Running Fence*—an 18-foot-tall white nylon curtain that zigzagged for 24 miles in northern California—from Highway 101 north of San Francisco to the Pacific Ocean.

After these successes, Christo was drawn to the urban environment. In 1983, he created *Surrounded Islands*. This project called for surrounding eleven islands in Miami, Florida's Biscayne Bay with 6.5 million square feet of pink plastic fabric. Where the installation of *Running Fences* required only the permission of the ranch-ers whose land was crossed by the fence, getting permission for *Surrounded Islands* took months of work. Meanwhile, a computer was used to design the shape of each individual section of the wrapping. Dozens of workers stitched the fabric. When everything was ready, over 1,500 anchors were set in place and a large crew worked for six days to wrap the islands. Exactly two weeks later, all the wrappings were removed, and the islands were restored to their original condition.

For years Christo had wanted to wrap a large public building. He realized this dream in 1995 when he wrapped the entire German Reichstag, or parliament building, in Berlin. *Wrapped Reichstag* required more than one million square feet of custom-made shiny, synthetic fabric that was held in place by more than nine miles of bright blue rope. Two weeks later, the wrapping was removed. Not a trace remains.

Christo's work has always sparked controversy. And that's just the way he wants it. However, more likely than not, his detractors are won over by the new vision of the world he presents. Environmentalists who oppose his projects are reassured by the research and the care that go into each of his designs. If you ever see one of Christo's creations, look quickly—it won't be there long, but it will change the way you see the world.

1. Christo designs his works of art to
   a. be permanent.
   b. last only a short time.
   c. please everyone.
   d. hide the faults of nature.

2. The word in paragraph 2 that means *huge* is _____.

3. The words "parliament building" in paragraph 4 refer to _____.

4. While it is not directly stated, the article suggests that
   a. people don't know much about art.
   b. it is easier to wrap an island than a building.
   c. art can appear in surprising forms.

5. Christo wrapped a mile of the Australian coast in order to
   a. protest against polluting the coastline.
   b. create a new cliff.
   c. make Australians angry.

6. On the whole, the article tells about
   a. how to wrap packages.
   b. how silly modern art is.
   c. how an artist can change the way we see the world.

7. Which statement does this article lead you to believe?
   a. Art forms change from time to time.
   b. Museum masterpieces are the only true art form.
   c. Christo doesn't want people to like his art.

8. Why does Christo remove his art after a short time?
   a. He needs the materials to use in his next project.
   b. The authorities will not grant permission for more than two weeks.
   c. He wants to show the special beauty of things that are not permanent.

9. Think about the concept for this group of articles. Which statement seems true both for the article and for the concept?
   a. Museums object to Christo's style of art.
   b. An artist can use the environment to create a new kind of art.
   c. Christo's projects pose serious threats to the environment.

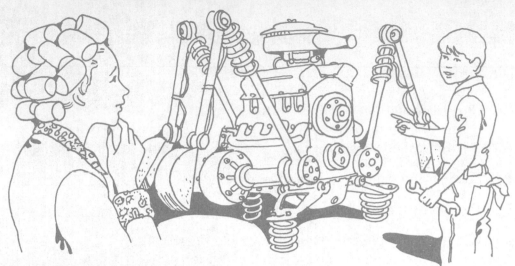

The Remarkable Thermothrockle

Sometimes, when everything is quiet, Harry Heimer goes out into the back yard and stares at the petunia patch. If he listens carefully, he thinks he can hear something rumbling underground. Then Harry has a feeling of real accomplishment. "That old Thermothrockle is still going," he says. "I wonder where it is now."

It all began one day last winter when Harry was in the library. He had asked the librarian for several back issues of *Popular Mechanics Magazine*. Harry was planning to build his own stereo amplifier and was looking for directions.

Tucked into one of the old magazines was a drawing on a wrinkled sheet of paper. It appeared to be of some kind of a mechanical invention.

"What a weird-looking thing," Harry thought. It reminded him of the pictures of those unmanned devices which space scientists had landed on the moon to scoop up samples of soil. It had several hinged arms and legs.

Harry studied the sheet carefully. There seemed to be nothing very difficult about assembling the device. In fact, Harry decided, any boy who had ever tinkered with an Erector set could probably do it.

Harry was puzzled by a note penciled beneath the drawing. It said, "Rejected by U.S. Patent Office as impossible."

Harry might have put the paper back, but he couldn't remember which issue it had been in. It was probably of no value to anyone anyway, Harry told himself. He tucked it into his own notebook and took it home, where he put it in the top drawer of his desk.

Now Harry was not one of those boys who goes out for sports. He never played Little League baseball or entered the annual Golden Gloves tournament. When swimming season came, Harry had other things to do. The "other things" were visits to junk yards. Harry loved junk. His idea of a good time was to take a sandwich and spend the day down at Sam's junk yard. Old Sam was a friend of Harry's and allowed him to come and go as he pleased.

During Harry's frequent visits to Sam's place, he collected various things that he might use in building the invention. He had no idea what the invention was. He had no idea what it would do. For lack of a better name, he referred to it in his own mind as the Thermothrockle. He didn't know what a Thermothrockle was, but the word had a nice solid sound to it.

Each of the parts Harry brought home he put in a pile in the back yard beside the garage. The pile of parts began to grow bigger and bigger. Harry's father threatened to call Sam to come and pick up his junk.

"Just leave it alone, please, Dad," Harry would say. "I'm going to build something."

"Yes, but what?" Mr. Heimer wanted to know.

"Yes, and when?" his mother asked. "You've got the junk lying right over the place where I grow my petunias. It's almost time to plant them."

As spring came on, the pile of junk grew bigger. Mrs. Heimer complained often, but Harry didn't seem to hear.

At last, one Saturday morning in May, Harry had the urge to begin to build. The Thermothrockle went together very easily. When it was about half finished, Harry's old enemy Horace Beeson strolled down the alley. Horace leered at the invention.

"Building a perpetual motion machine, aren't you, Harry?" he said. "I can tell. I've built dozens of them. And I can tell you something else, Harry. They don't work!"

For a moment, Harry was upset. He knew better than to try to build a perpetual motion machine. People had been trying to build perpetual motion machines for centuries. You could read about them in the encyclopedia. They were machines that were supposed to operate forever. They would never run down. Of course, no one had ever succeeded in building one. It was the mark of a real bird-brain—like Horace—to even try such a thing. Since it had never occurred to Harry that his Thermothrockle might be a perpetual motion machine, he ignored Horace.

Mike, down the street, also came to watch. Mike was several years younger than Harry, but he was Harry's friend—always a bit grubby with a runny nose, but a good kid, nevertheless. Sometimes Mike helped Harry, but usually he just sat on the fence and watched. Harry's family did not share Harry's appreciation of Mike. The other Heimers thought Mike was a nuisance and not very bright. He didn't speak plainly and they couldn't understand him.

"What is that thing?" Harry's older sister asked one morning. She had come into the yard to dry her hair in the sun. Harry looked at her head, which was covered with big rollers.

"I haven't told anyone else, Eleanor," he said, "but you might as well know. It's a hair-curling machine."

"You're not very funny, Harry Heimer!" stormed Eleanor. "And I might add that if you spent a little more time on your own appearance, it would be a big improvement."

With one greasy hand, Harry pushed the hair out of his eyes and went on with his work. The Thermothrockle was almost finished. After Eleanor left, Harry bolted the last part into place.

Immediately, the machine began to vibrate. It shook violently and clawed at the ground. Harry was frightened. He quickly unbolted the last part he had attached and the Thermothrockle once again stood motionless.

Harry sat back on his heels to think things over. Perhaps this *was* a perpetual motion machine after all—and a self-starting one, at that. If the Thermothrockle was going to work so well, he wanted to be ready. Perhaps he should have a small ceremony or at least an official observer, someone he could trust.

Harry went to look for Mike. He found him in his kitchen making a sandwich. The small boy followed Harry home.

"Just sit on the fence and watch, Mike," Harry said. "When they test a new airplane, they always have a second pilot in a chase plane watching. Your job is to observe."

"O.K.," said Mike agreeably.

The Thermothrockle was too heavy for Harry to move. It stood near the place where the junk had been—by the garage, in Mrs. Heimer's petunia bed.

"Get ready," said Harry.

"I'm ready," said Mike calmly eating his peanut-butter-and-jelly sandwich. "Do you want a countdown?"

"That's not necessary," said Harry. Gingerly he bolted the final part back into place. At once, there was a whirring and a clanking noise. Mike, startled, fell off the fence backward as the Thermothrockle began to dig. The hinged legs clawed the soil and tossed it into three neat piles. By the time Mike had picked himself up, the Thermothrockle was inside a hole twelve inches deep.

"It's a mechanical mole," Mike announced. "What makes it go?"

"I don't know," said Harry. "And look what it's doing now. It's pulling the dirt into the hole behind it!"

The hinged arms were reaching up to the three piles of dirt. They scooped up the soil and scattered it smoothly over the top of the Thermothrockle. Just before the machine disappeared, one claw reached out and snatched the wrinkled paper on which the plan was drawn.

Mike laughed loudly. "It dug a hole, climbed in, and now it's covered itself up!"

The whirring and clanking machine was out of sight. The earth quivered and shook as the Thermothrockle moved deeper under the petunia bed.

"Maybe I should stop it," said Harry. He ran into the garage for a shovel. He dug frantically for a few minutes then quit. "It's no use, I can't catch up with it."

Just then Harry's mother came into the yard. "Harry," she scolded, "I wish you'd answer when I call you. I've been calling you for five minutes." She paused as she saw Harry with the shovel. "Why how nice, Harry, you've spaded up the flower bed!"

From his perch on the fence, Mike explained. "The Thermothrockle did it."

Mrs. Heimer looked at Mike's jelly-smeared face and shuddered slightly. She wished that boy would clean himself up and learn to speak plainly. She glanced back at the flower bed. For a moment she felt a little dizzy. It looked as if the earth were moving.

"You've even gotten rid of all that junk, Harry. Thank you. This year," she went on, "I think I'll have red petunias."

But Harry wasn't listening. The Thermothrockle had disappeared, taking the plan with it. He knew that he would never be able to build another one.

1246 words

II

Some Changes Are Planned; Others Are Accidental

In this section, you will read about two different ways in which things change. You will read about these things in the areas of history, biology, anthropology, economics, geography, Earth science, mathematics, engineering, and art.

Keep these questions in mind when you are reading.

1. What are some changes that have been planned?

2. What are some changes that have come by accident?

3. To be good, does a change have to be planned?

4. Are people affected by both kinds of change? How?

5. In what ways do you adjust to various changes?

Look on pages 7-9 for help with words you don't understand in this section.

The Long Exile

Israel is one of the world's youngest nations, but its people have a long history. The Jews, or Hebrews, first settled on the narrow strip of land at the eastern end of the Mediterranean Sea about 3,500 years ago. They lost this homeland in Roman times and did not get it back again until 1948, when the State of Israel was established. Roman soldiers conquered the Jews in 63 B.C., and their land became a Roman province called Judea. Again and again, the Jews rebelled and tried to throw out the conquerors. Finally, in A.D. 133, the Romans ended all resistance by killing many of the Jews and forcing most of the others to leave the country. The Jews who survived were scattered over Europe and Asia. They began a long period of exile.

Wherever they lived, the Jews carefully preserved their religion and laws, their language and customs. They dreamed of their homeland and planned for the day when they could return to it. They had to wait nearly 2,000 years.

Meanwhile, Arabs, Turks, and European Crusaders warred over the Jewish homeland, which came to be known as Palestine. After 1917, Palestine was ruled by Great Britain, though the population was largely Arab. The British allowed Jews to resettle in Palestine if they wished to, and thousands took advantage of this opportunity. The Arabs resented this, and they fought to keep the Jews out. There was constant friction among British, Arabs, and Jews.

Finally, after World War II, Great Britain asked the United Nations to find some solution to the problem. The plan that was adopted, in 1947, called for dividing Palestine into two states, one Arab and the other Jewish. The Arab state became a part of neighboring Jordan. The Jewish state became Israel, the first new nation established under United Nations supervision.

1. The land of Israel was once called
    a. Poland.   c. Persia.
    b. Palestine.   d. Palisades.

2. The word in paragraph 4 that means *rubbing* or *clashing over viewpoint* is

    _____ .

3. The words "a part of neighboring Jordan" in the last paragraph describe the

    _____   _____ .

4. While it is not directly stated, the article suggests that
    a. Arabs and Turks resented the British because they had no religion.
    b. the Jewish religion is one of the world's oldest living religions.
    c. religion did not start until the Crusaders went to Palestine.

5. The province called Judea was ruled by the
    a. Russians.
    b. Romans.
    c. Rumanians.

6. On the whole, the article tells about
    a. the eastern end of the Mediterranean Sea in 1917.
    b. the United Nations after the Second World War.
    c. the history of the Jews and their homeland.

7. Which statement does this article lead you to believe?
    a. People's dreams can survive for centuries.
    b. It is foolish to keep your dreams alive.
    c. A young nation cannot have a long history.

8. Why did the Jews rebel against the Romans?
    a. They wanted to protest against Roman customs.
    b. They wanted to throw out their conquerors.
    c. They wanted to have Turks rule them instead.

9. Think about the concept for this group of articles. Which statement seems true both for the article and for the concept?
    a. The United Nations helped plan the creation of other new nations.
    b. There is no room for any more new nations in the world of today.
    c. Israel is the only new nation the United Nations ever created.

The Luck of Cortez

In 1519, Hernando Cortez marched into central Mexico with an army of 400 men. A year later, this bearded Spaniard and his small force had conquered the mighty Aztec Indian Empire. The Spaniards had superior weapons and they possessed horses, which the Aztecs had never seen before. But that is only part of the story.

Cortez arrived in Mexico during the same year that the Aztecs expected their god Quetzalcoatl (Ket säl′ kwät′ əl) to return. Montezuma, the Aztec ruler, concluded that Cortez was the god Quetzalcoatl. Instead of fighting the Spaniards, the Aztecs welcomed Cortez and his army.

Quetzalcoatl was supposed to have been a human leader of the Aztec people as well as the god they called the Plumed Serpent. In human form, Quetzalcoatl had been a fair-skinned, bearded man who had taught his people such practical skills as farming, building, and metal-working. Then he had sailed away across the eastern sea. Before embarking, he had told the Aztecs he would return in the year 1-Reed. The year that was 1-Reed on the Aztec calendar was 1519 on the European calendar.

Among the messengers who came with gifts of welcome was a young woman, Ce Malinalli. She approached the man the natives believed to be a god. She dressed him in the color black, without telling him that wearing black was the mark of a god. It seems that she had special plans to make Cortez's arrival as magical as possible, without informing him at all. She saw herself as the companion to this conqueror.

She persuaded Cortez not to land as soon as he arrived but to wait until full daylight on the magical day of the year.

Eventually, she traveled at the conqueror's side, as the wise Doña Marina, translating Cortez' every word. After welcoming the strangers, the Aztecs lost 120,000 to 240,000 of their people to the Spaniards. No wonder the natives gave her the name of "princess of suffering."

Cortez was a clever and resourceful soldier, but unplanned circumstances helped him. Because of an accident of history, Cortez the Conqueror was greeted as a god of culture, civilization, and kindness.

1. Quetzalcoatl was a leader of the
   a. Austrians.
   b. Asians.
   c. Aztecs.
   d. Amazons.

2. The word in paragraph 4 that means *one who wins in war* is _____.

3. The words "a clever and resourceful soldier" in the last paragraph describe

   _____ .

4. While it is not directly stated, the article suggests that
   a. Cortez was a god who came to the Aztecs as a plumed serpent.
   b. Cortez spread culture, civilization, and kindness in Mexico.
   c. Cortez destroyed a civilization without need or cause.

5. Something the Aztecs had never seen before were the Spaniards'
   a. horses.
   b. beards.
   c. feathers.

6. On the whole, the article tells about
   a. an accident of history that ended a civilization.
   b. the year on the Aztec calendar known as 1-Reed.
   c. the plumes that Hernando Cortez wore on his helmet.

7. Which statement does this article lead you to believe?
   a. Cortez is remembered in history as the man who saved the Aztec Empire.
   b. The Spaniards had no respect for the great Aztec culture.
   c. Conquerors usually have fair skins and beards and plumed helmets.

8. Why did Ce Malinalli help Cortez dress like a god?
   a. She thought she could become the companion of the conqueror.
   b. The messengers told her a secret about the gods.
   c. Montezuma had chosen her to welcome Cortez.

9. Think about the concept for this group of articles. Which statement seems true both for the article and for the concept?
   a. What will be, will be.
   b. What we don't know can hurt us.
   c. What we don't know can't hurt us.

Learning About Mars and Venus

Mars and Venus are the planets nearest Earth. For many centuries, people have been eager to learn more about these close neighbors in our solar system. Since the Space Age began, scientists have built new tools to expand their knowledge of Mars and Venus. The most important of these tools are unmanned spacecraft called planetary probes.

Mariner 2, launched by the U.S. National Aeronautics and Space Administration (NASA) in 1962, was the first probe to return information about Venus. This probe passed within 21,500 miles of Venus. It reported the temperature of the planet to be about 800°F. In 1970, the Soviet planetary probe *Venera 7* was the first spacecraft to land on the surface of Venus and transmit information back to Earth. In 1978, NASA sent two more probes to Venus. *Pioneer Venus 1* and *Pioneer Venus 2* sent back photographs and information about the weather and atmosphere.

Mariner 4, launched by NASA in 1964, was the first probe to return information about Mars. It took photographs as it passed within 6,200 miles of the planet. In 1976, *Viking 1* and *Viking 2* landed on the surface of Mars. The Viking probes transmitted the first close-up pictures of Mars back to Earth. These probes also studied the soil and atmosphere on Mars.

Because of budget cutbacks, no more probes were sent for almost twenty years. Then at the end of 1996, NASA launched the *Mars Pathfinder*. After a seven-month journey, *Pathfinder* landed on Mars on July 4, 1997. It was the first probe to land on Mars without first going into orbit around the planet.

Pathfinder carried with it a roving robotic exploration vehicle called *Sojourner*. *Sojourner* was two feet long and one foot tall and had six spiked wheels. It used lasers to navigate and could travel 80 feet per hour. One of *Sojourner*'s main tasks was to collect information that might tell scientists whether the water necessary for life had ever existed on Mars.

While *Sojourner* studied rock and soil samples, *Pathfinder* transmitted three-dimensional pictures of Mars back to Earth. These photographs were sent to 25 different sites on the Internet; NASA's Web site, alone, was viewed by an estimated 15 million Earthlings.

1. The planets nearest Earth are
    a. Saturn and Neptune.
    b. Pluto and Uranus.
    c. Jupiter and Mars.
    d. Mars and Venus.

2. The word in paragraph 1 that means *instruments used to explore or examine* is
    _____.

3. The words "roving robotic exploration vehicle" in paragraph 5 describe
    _____.

4. While it is not directly stated, the article suggests that
    a. people keep adding to their information about the planets.
    b. the planets are too far away for people to learn anything.
    c. information about the planets is not very accurate.

5. The first probe to return information about Venus was
    a. *Mariner 2.*
    b. *Viking 1.*
    c. *Pathfinder.*

6. On the whole, the article tells about
    a. taking satellite pictures of Earth's surface.
    b. Studying the planets nearest Earth.
    c. the different names used for unmanned space probes.

7. Which statement does this article lead you to believe?
    a. People probably cannot exist in the atmosphere of Venus.
    b. Most scientists believe that human beings are living on Venus now.
    c. Mars is much closer to Earth than Venus is.

8. Why were no probes sent to Mars between 1976 and 1996?
    a. NASA needed time to study the results of the first probes.
    b. NASA was sending probes to Mercury during that time.
    c. NASA's budget had been cut.

9. Think about the concept for this group of articles. Which statement seems true both for the article and for the concept?
    a. Spacecraft from other planets may soon visit Earth.
    b. Scientists plan to probe other planets in our solar system as soon as possible.
    c. Only unmanned spacecraft can visit other planets.

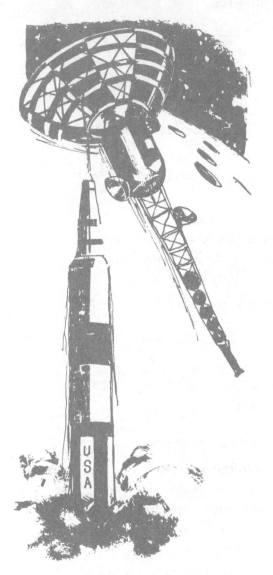

Explorer 1 *Saves the Day*

Explorer 1 was an artificial earth satellite designed and constructed in a hurry. It was launched by a rocket that was the second choice of scientists planning the first United States space effort. Yet *Explorer 1* made one of the greatest scientific discoveries of all time.

The project that was supposed to launch America's first artificial satellite into earth orbit was named Vanguard. On October 4, 1957, the Vanguard satellite was nearly ready for testing. But on that date, Russian scientists launched the world's first artificial satellite, *Sputnik 1*. The United States was surprised and disappointed to find itself behind in the space race. Work on the Vanguard project was speeded up. The launching was set for December 6. On that day, millions of television viewers saw the Vanguard rocket rise a few feet, then fall back and explode into flames.

An urgent call went out to Dr. Wernher von Braun, whose space research team was working on another rocket named Jupiter C. How soon could Jupiter C be ready to boost a new satellite into orbit?

About eight weeks later, on January 31, 1958, a Jupiter C rocket successfully placed in earth orbit the first United States artificial satellite, *Explorer 1*. Packed with scientific instruments, *Explorer 1* had been hastily constructed and weighed only 30 pounds. Yet *Explorer 1* sent back to earth more important information than had *Sputnik 2*, launched about the same time but thirty-six times heavier.

The most important information provided by *Explorer 1* indicated that a belt of intense radiation surrounded the earth. Dr. James A. Van Allen studied this information. He soon began mapping the radiation belt that now bears his name.

The fiery accident on the launch pad had made *Explorer 1*, rather than *Vanguard*, America's first satellite. Even more surprising, *Explorer 1* discovered the Van Allen radiation belt.

FIND THE ANSWERS

1. The world's first artificial satellite was named
   - a. *Sputnik 1*.
   - b. *Lika*.
   - c. *Explorer 1*.
   - d. *Vanguard*.

2. The word in paragraph 1 that means *made* or *built* is

   _____ .

3. The words "Packed with scientific instruments" in paragraph 4 describe the

   _____ .

4. While it is not directly stated, the article suggests that
   - a. Russia has brilliant scientists.
   - b. Americans are the best scientists.
   - c. there are scientists in only two countries.

5. America's first satellite was supposed to be the
   - a. *Uranus*.
   - b. *Vanguard*.
   - c. *Jupiter*.

6. On the whole, the article tells about
   - a. an American satellite which made an important discovery.
   - b. the launching of a satellite which failed to take off.
   - c. the different weights needed for all the satellites.

7. Which statement does this article lead you to believe?
   - a. Both Russia and the United States have given up space programs.
   - b. The Vanguard and Sputnik satellites were the only ones launched.
   - c. More artificial satellites have been launched since 1957.

8. Why was the United States surprised and disappointed when *Sputnik 1* was launched?
   - a. We were disappointed to hear there were scientists in Russia.
   - b. We were upset to find ourselves behind in the space race.
   - c. We were surprised at the name chosen for a space satellite.

9. Think about the concept for this group of articles. Which statement seems true both for the article and for the concept?
   - a. No one pays any attention to a discovery if it is not made on purpose.
   - b. Scientists do not approve of discoveries that are accidental.
   - c. Sometimes, unexpected accidents can change a scientific program.

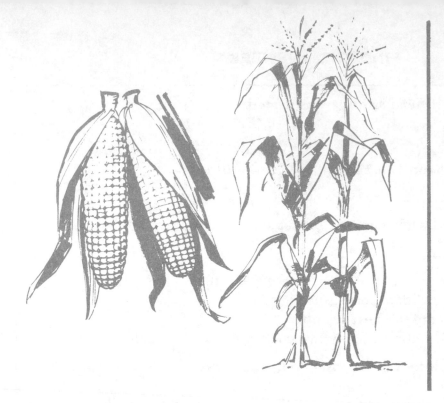

Fuel in the Cornfield

Gasoline is one of the most important fuels used in transportation. Its widespread use began in the early 1900s with the mass production of automobiles. Its use grew consistently during the twentieth century, and will continue to do so well into the twenty-first century. However, the world's supply of oil, or petroleum—from which gasoline is derived—is limited. If we continue to consume oil at the present rate, we will run out in a few decades. Clearly we need alternatives to gasoline.

One such alternative already exists. Ethanol is a fuel made from grains. While ethanol can be made from corn, wheat, soy beans, or sugar beets, almost 90% of the ethanol produced in the United States is made from corn.

The production of ethanol from corn is a multistep process. First starch is extracted from the corn kernels. The starch is then turned into a simple sugar. Finally, the sugar is fermented to produce ethanol.

Today, ethanol is still more expensive to produce than gasoline. And cars are not yet equipped to run on pure ethanol. However, a blend of three parts ethanol to seven parts gasoline works perfectly well in the average automobile. In addition, gasoline mixed with ethanol has been shown to produce fewer toxic emissions, which pollute the atmosphere.

Not only is ethanol good for the oil supply, it is good for the economy. Ethanol was first made during the 1970s. The use of corn for ethanol production jumped from 25 million bushels of corn in 1975 to 515 million bushels in 1995. Currently the United States is the world leader in ethanol production. As an example of how important ethanol has become to our economy, ethanol production in the mid-1990s accounted for 17% of all the corn grown in the state of Illinois.

Ethanol will not only lessen our dependence on oil as an energy source, but it will also create new jobs, improve the economy, and reduce pollution.

1. One alternative to gasoline is
   a. petroleum.   c. ethanol.
   b. toxic emissions.   d. starch.

2. The word in paragraph 2 that means *something used in place of something else* is _____.

3. The words "which pollute the atmosphere" in paragraph 4 describe _____ _____.

4. While it is not directly stated, the article suggests that
   a. automobile engines are largely responsible for air pollution.
   b. oil producing nations will soon convert to farming.
   c. air pollution will be eliminated by the beginning of the twenty-first century.

5. Almost 90% of ethanol is made from
   a. soy beans.
   b. sugar beets.
   c. corn.

6. On the whole, the article tells about
   a. the income of American farmers.
   b. reducing pollution.
   c. the development of one form of alternative fuel.

7. Which statement does this article lead you to believe?
   a. The development of alternative fuel is a waste of time.
   b. The development of alternative fuel is essential.
   c. Other countries should grow more corn.

8. Why is ethanol blended with gasoline?
   a. Cars are not yet equipped to run on pure ethanol.
   b. The blend of ethanol and gasoline makes engines run faster.
   c. The blending process creates new jobs.

9. Think about the concept for this group of articles. Which statement seems true both for the article and for the concept?
   a. Soon corn will be used only to produce alternative fuel.
   b. We will never be able to control pollution.
   c. To change our reliance on gasoline as an energy source will take careful planning.

Runaway Plant

Visitors to the New Orleans Cotton Exposition of 1884 saw a new tropical plant that had been brought from Venezuela. The new plant floated on the surface of a pond or stream, supported by an air-filled bladder in the stalk of each leaf. Each plant bore clusters of very beautiful orchidlike blossoms.

Some exposition visitors obtained cuttings of the plant to take home with them because they wanted the beautiful, pale-violet flowers floating on their garden pools. They got what they wanted and more, for the water hyacinth escaped from cultivation and soon became a troublesome weed. Today, it chokes many streams and rivers in the southern United States, from Florida west to Texas.

Water hyacinths grow very quickly, covering the surface of a stream from bank to bank. One plant can produce 1,000 more plants in less than two months. The plants often form a tangled mass so thick that a boat can't force a way through it.

In the United States, a great deal of money has been spent on projects designed to control water hyacinths. Poisons will kill the plants and dredges can scoop them out of the water, but they soon reappear. Some scientists have suggested establishing the manatee, or sea cow, in the afflicted regions. The manatee is a large aquatic mammal that can consume up to 100 pounds of vegetation a day, and it will eat water hyacinths.

But since the manatees are endangered, it is unlikely that they will provide a permanent solution. Therefore, scientists are trying to discover uses for the water hyacinth. Some researchers are experimenting with using dried water hyacinths as livestock feed. Others are experimenting with using these plants in water purification systems because water hyacinths can absorb many chemicals, including industrial wastes.

Today, people try to be more careful about importing alien plants than they were in 1884. Even so, no way has yet been found to control this beautiful plant and other plant pests, such as milfoil, that clog so many waterways.

1. The water hyacinth was brought to New Orleans from
   a. Venezuela.   c. Vancouver.
   b. Victoria.   d. Virginia.

2. The word in paragraph 1 that means *bunches or groups of the same kind of thing growing together* is _____.

3. The words "a tangled mass so thick that a boat can't force a way through it" in paragraph 3 describe the _____.

4. While it is not directly stated, the article suggests that
   a. nature can be too generous.
   b. nature is always controlled.
   c. there are no mistakes in nature.

5. Water hyacinths may be used to
   a. poison manatees.
   b. replace orchids.
   c. help purify water.

6. On the whole, the article tells about
   a. the difficulty in controlling a troublesome plant.
   b. a Cotton Exposition held in New Orleans in 1884.
   c. poisons and dredges used to kill certain plants.

7. Which statement does this article lead you to believe?
   a. Hyacinths were planted to choke rivers from bank to bank.
   b. Ships have no problem moving on rivers clogged with weeds.
   c. In 1884 no one knew very much about the water hyacinths.

8. Why did some scientists suggest establishing the manatee from Florida to Texas?
   a. Manatees will eat water hyacinths.
   b. Scientists like to experiment on manatees.
   c. Manatees are endangered.

9. Think about the concept for this group of articles. Which statement seems true both for the article and for the concept?
   a. There was no scientific planning for importing water hyacinth.
   b. Plans were made to clog the waterways with water hyacinths.
   c. A weed cannot be troublesome if it has beautiful blossoms.

The Leakeys' African Discoveries

Dr. Louis S. B. Leakey (1903–1972) was born in East Africa. As a boy he roamed the wild bush country of Kenya with young African tribesmen. From time to time, he would find odd-shaped stones, which he identified as the tools and weapons of prehistoric beings.

When Leakey was older, he was sent to England to finish his education. He informed one teacher, who had inquired about his plans for the future, that he planned to search for evidence of human ancestors in Africa. The teacher told him to go to Asia instead. No one expected important discoveries to be made in Africa. But Leakey was the kind of person who believed in himself and in the evidence he had gathered as a boy.

Leakey returned to Africa to continue his work. There he concentrated on Olduvai Gorge in Tanzania, a large nation just south of Kenya. He chose Olduvai Gorge because it was rich in fossil remains.

Leakey married a trained archeologist, Mary Nicol. Together, these great fossil hunters found thousands of crude stone tools. They unearthed the fossil bones of extinct animals that prehistoric humans had killed and eaten. Then in 1959, Mary Leakey discovered the kind of fossil they had been hoping to find. It was the skull of a humanlike creature that lived 1 3/4 million years ago. This important fossil skull proved that some of our earliest ancestors had lived in Africa. In 1978, she found fossilized footprints which indicate that our

ancestors were walking upright as early as 3 1/2 million years ago.

Louis and Mary Leakey's son Richard, born in 1944, followed in the family tradition. Trained as a scientist, Richard Leakey discovered many humanlike fossils near Lake Turkana in Kenya. Richard's wife Meave, born in 1942, is a paleontologist. She leads teams of researchers and helps identify the fossils they uncover.

The discoveries made by this amazing family have helped convince scientists that Africa, rather than Asia, may have been the first home of human beings.

70

1. A large nation just south of Kenya is called
   a. Turkey.
   c. Thailand.
   b. Tanzania.
   d. Tasmania.

2. The word in paragraph 5 that means *went on with* is _____.

3. The words "the tools and weapons of prehistoric beings" in paragraph 1 describe the odd-shaped _____.

4. While it is not directly stated, the article suggests that
   a. scientists once believed that the earliest humans lived in Asia.
   b. scientists were once very much against archeologists.
   c. scientists never take anybody's advice.

5. The Leakeys found thousands of crude stone tools at
   a. Kenyan valleys.
   b. East Asia.
   c. Olduvai Gorge.

6. On the whole, the article tells about
   a. Dr. Louis Leakey's important teacher in England.
   b. the Leakeys' search for the oldest known ancestors to humans.
   c. the marriage of Dr. Leakey to a trained archeologist.

7. Which statement does this article lead you to believe?
   a. Louis Leakey convinced scientists that he could make crude tools.
   b. Louis Leakey should have gone to Asia as he was advised to do.
   c. Louis Leakey had the courage to follow his own convictions.

8. Why was Louis Leakey sent to England?
   a. He was sent there to finish his education.
   b. He was sent there to find prehistoric life.
   c. He was sent there to learn about Africa.

9. Think about the concept for this group of articles. Which statement seems true both for the article and for the concept?
   a. The Leakeys lived many millions of years ago.
   b. The Leakeys' research has always followed a definite plan.
   c. It was an accident that led Louis Leakey to Africa.

The Vanished Mandans

In the early 1800s, about 1,500 Mandan Indians lived in permanent villages along the upper Missouri River. In 1837 a steamboat came up the river, and white settlers visited the villages. Shortly thereafter, only thirty-one Mandans were left alive.

There had been no battle. It was not the enemies' guns that killed the Mandans, but an infectious disease against which the Indians had no resistance. Two of the outsiders who had visited the Mandan villages had been sick with smallpox.

The Mandans were the first of many Indian tribes to suffer from the great smallpox epidemic that swept the western plains between 1837 and 1841. The Mandans are of particular importance because they were among the most advanced of the Plains Indians. They hunted buffalo, but they also farmed, raising corn, beans, pumpkins, and sunflowers.

They built circular log houses forty to sixty feet in diameter, much larger and sturdier than most Indian dwellings.

Several Mandan families shared a house, but for privacy, each family had a curtained-off space near the outer walls. The Mandans had their own legends and ceremonials, and they made pottery and unusually handsome baskets.

This way of life disappeared with the Mandans in 1837.

The smallpox spread to the neighboring villages of the Arikari and Hidatsa Indians, where about half the 4,000 inhabitants died. Then the disease spread to the nomadic Plains Indians who lived farther west. It struck the Blackfeet, the Crow, the Sioux, the Pawnee, the Osage, the Kiowa, and the Comanche.

How many Indians died of smallpox? No one will ever know, as no records were kept. But many tribes lost half their people. By accident, the western Indians were half-defeated before United States soldiers set out to conquer them.

1. The Mandans were among the most advanced of the
   a. River Indians.   c. Eastern Indians.
   b. Plains Indians.   d. Desert Indians.

2. The word in paragraph 2 that means *spreading from one person to another* is

   _____ .

3. The words "forty to sixty feet in diameter" in paragraph 3 describe the

   _____ _____ .

4. While it is not directly stated, the article suggests that
   a. it is not possible for one people to spread disease to others.
   b. civilization does not always benefit a primitive people.
   c. primitive people need to be exposed to many diseases.

5. Two visitors to the Mandan villages had been sick with
   a. measles.
   b. chickenpox.
   c. smallpox.

6. On the whole, the article tells about
   a. Indians who had ceremonials and legends.
   b. the destruction of a people through disease.
   c. the number of inhabitants in Mandan villages.

7. Which statement does this article lead you to believe?
   a. Infectious diseases become epidemics only among Indian tribes.
   b. The Mandan Indians refused to take medicine to help them get well.
   c. There was no way to control infectious diseases in the 1800s.

8. Why did the Mandans' way of life disappear?
   a. They were wiped out by stampeding buffalo.
   b. The baskets they made did not sell.
   c. Most of the people died of a smallpox epidemic.

9. Think about the concept for this group of articles. Which statement seems true both for the article and for the concept?
   a. The settlers did not purposely infect the Indians with a disease.
   b. The settlers were anxious to share their disease with the Indians.
   c. The Indians should have planned to be away when the settlers came.

A New Flag for an Old Colony

Great Britain occupied Hong Kong Island at the beginning of the Opium War, a war with China over trade disputes. When China lost that war in 1842, it turned Hong Kong over to the British. In 1860, China also turned over the nearby peninsula of the mainland and another island to the British. Then, in 1898, China leased an adjacent area of the Chinese mainland known as the New Territories to Great Britain for 99 years. This entire 415-square-mile area in southeastern China became the British colony of Hong Kong.

Over the years, Hong Kong became a thriving manufacturing center for such things as fabric, clothing, plastics, electronics, jewelry, and toys. It was known the world over for its reliable banking and shipping services.

After World War II, China wanted Hong Kong back. The new communist Chinese government maintained that the treaties that had given Great Britain control over Hong Kong were not valid. The 99-year lease on the new Territories would expire in 1997. When that lease expired, China wanted all of Hong Kong back.

After years of diplomatic discussions, an agreement was reached in 1984. That year, the Joint Declaration on Hong Kong, signed by Great Britain and China, spelled out the terms under which all of Hong Kong would be returned to China when the lease on the New Territories expired. First a new constitution, the Basic Law, was written for Hong Kong. The Basic Law allows Hong Kong to keep its capitalist economy and some of its former freedoms for a period of 50 years. This unusual arrangement of a communist country allowing one area to remain capitalist was devised by former Chinese leader Deng Ziaoping. He called it the "one country, two systems" plan.

Many people feared protests between Hong Kong's pro-democracy movement and communist authorities, but the transition went smoothly. At midnight on June 30, 1997, the British flag was lowered and the Chinese and Hong Kong flags were raised. One hundred and fifty-five years of British rule came to an end, and Hong Kong entered a new era. The world watches to see if the one country, two systems plan will work.

1. Deng Ziaoping devised the
   - a. lease for the New Territories.
   - c. new Hong Kong flag.
   - b. one country, two systems plan.
   - d. Opium War.

2. The word in paragraph 1 that means *lying next to* is _____.

3. The words "a war with China over trade disputes" in paragraph 1 describe the
   _____ _____.

4. While it is not directly stated, the article suggests that
   - a. Hong Kong may face problems in the future.
   - b. The people in Hong Kong were unhappy under British rule.
   - c. Hong Kong wants to become an independent communist country.

5. Great Britain had a lease on the New Territories for
   - a. 50 years.
   - b. 99 years.
   - c. 156 years.

6. On the whole, the article tells about
   - a. the causes of the Opium War.
   - b. the reasons for Hong Kong's thriving economy.
   - c. Hong Kong's transition from British to Chinese rule.

7. Which statement does this article lead you to believe?
   - a. Manufacturing centers in Hong Kong will be shut down.
   - b. Hong Kong will have to go through a period of adjustment.
   - c. The capital of China will be moved to Hong Kong.

8. Why did China turn Hong Kong over to Great Britain?
   - a. Great Britain defeated China in the Opium War.
   - b. Great Britain defeated China in World War II.
   - c. Great Britain needed a good harbor for its ships.

9. Think about the concept for this group of articles. Which statement seems true both for the article and for the concept?
   - a. Winning a war is a good way to gain territory.
   - b. The people of Hong Kong prefer to be ruled by outsiders.
   - c. The outcome of a planned change is not always immediately evident.

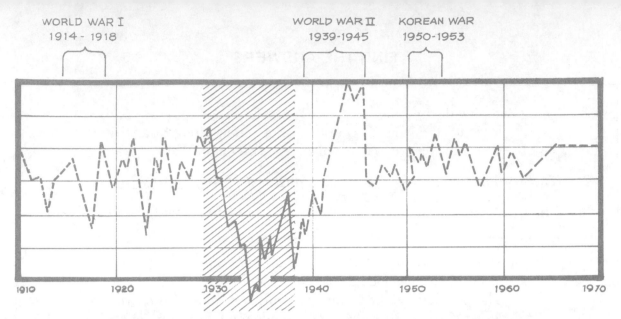

WORLD WAR I
1914 - 1918

WORLD WAR II
1939-1945

KOREAN WAR
1950-1953

1910   1920   1930   1940   1950   1960   1970

THE GREAT DEPRESSION BEGINNING 1929

Boom to Bust, 1929 to 1933

For most people in the United States, the 1920s were years of comfort, easy credit, and easy money. The stock market crash of October, 1929, was one event that changed the good times into hard times.

In the late 1920s, nearly everyone was certain that the easy credit and the good times would go on and on. Many were so confident that they borrowed from banks to buy cars, new homes, new furniture, clothing, and shares of stock in the ownership of America's big businesses. The stock market became a gambling place.

As long as stock prices went up, people could sell their stock shares at a profit and pay back what they had borrowed. But when stock prices fell, even a little, things changed. The banks demanded their money. To pay their debts, the borrowers had to sell their stocks for whatever they could get.

When a great many people have to sell stocks and few are eager to buy, stock prices plunge rapidly—and that is what happened in 1929.

Suddenly, people were less confident of the future. Many panicked and sold their stock shares. They stopped buying homes, cars, and furniture. Some factories had to close and many factory employees lost their jobs. Many stock shares became worthless. The Great Depression had begun.

People could not pay the banks the money they had borrowed, and the banks could not operate without money. Between 1930 and 1933, more than 9,000 banks closed. Many people lost their life savings.

Although the Great Depression affected the lives of millions of Americans, one after-effect was good. Laws were passed to insure wiser government control of stock transactions and banking procedures. Americans were determined not to undergo again the hard times of a severe depression.

76

FIND THE ANSWERS

1. The lives of millions of Americans were affected by the
   - a. Gay Succession.
   - c. Grave Recession.
   - b. Good Procession.
   - d. Great Depression.

2. The word in the last paragraph that means *ways of conducting a business* is

   _____ .

3. The words "a gambling place" in paragraph 2 describe the _____

   _____ .

4. While it is not directly stated, the article suggests that
   - a. gambling on the stock market did no one any harm.
   - b. people paid in advance for everything they bought.
   - c. people were not managing their money carefully.

5. Banks could not operate without
   - a. stocks.
   - b. money.
   - c. credit.

6. On the whole, the article tells about
   - a. Americans who want to undergo a severe depression.
   - b. people who passed laws to control the government.
   - c. the cause and effect of a stock market crash.

7. Which statement does this article lead you to believe?
   - a. The stock market crash ended hard times and brought good times.
   - b. The stock market crash affected people who did not own stocks.
   - c. The stock market crash only affected owners of certain stocks.

8. Why did borrowers have to sell their stocks?
   - a. They wanted to see the stocks go down.
   - b. They needed money to pay their debts.
   - c. They hoped to get rich quick.

9. Think about the concept for this group of articles. Which statement seems true both for the article and for the concept?
   - a. Stock prices that go up and down rapidly do not affect the economy.
   - b. It is good for the economy when factory employees lose work.
   - c. The need for controls in our economy was an unexpected lesson.

Frozen in Time

In the middle of the first century A.D., the Roman city of Pompeii flourished on the Bay of Naples less than a mile from the foot of Mount Vesuvius. At the time, Pompeii was a relatively unimportant Roman port, known more for its resorts than for its commercial importance to the empire.

Vesuvius had been quiet for so long that most people thought it was just another mountain. Those who knew it was a volcano probably believed it to be extinct. Then in A.D. 62, a severe earthquake struck the area and damaged buildings in Pompeii. However, residents of Italy were used to earthquakes and did not connect them with volcanic activity. Believing the danger to be over, Pompeians began to rebuild their city. The series of minor earthquakes that shook the region over the next 16 years did not seem to be a cause for alarm.

Then on August 24, A.D. 79, several extremely strong shocks were followed by an eruption so violent that it blew the top off Mount Vesuvius. For two days hot ashes, volcanic dust, and poisonous gases spewed forth, covering the surrounding countryside. The city of Pompeii was buried in hot ash to a depth of twelve feet.

Historians believe that most residents fled the city in the early hours of the eruption. Residents who, for whatever reason, stayed behind were killed by the poisonous gases or by the flow of hot ash. Their bodies were buried with their city.

Pompeii was almost forgotten until a local peasant discovered a buried wall while he was digging in a vineyard in 1748. Treasure hunters moved in immediately, but for more than a century, the digging was carried out in a hit-or-miss fashion. Then Giuseppe Fiorelli, who was in charge from 1860 to 1875, came up with a plan. It was his idea to dig out the city block by block and restore buildings, homes, and temples to their original places.

Today, about three-fourths of Pompeii has been uncovered. Many buildings have been restored—some even include a second story complete with balconies. Beautiful statues and even ancient graffiti have been unearthed. As a testament to Roman engineering, some fountains still work. The restored city is a life-size museum of Roman life as it was lived 2,000 years ago. Strangely, the eruption that destroyed Pompeii turned out to be the very force that preserved it.

1. Mount Vesuvius destroyed Pompeii in
       a. A.D. 62.   c. 1748.
       b. A.D. 79.   d. 1875.

2. The word in paragraph 6 that means *removed by digging* is

    _____.

3. The words "a relatively unimportant Roman port" in paragraph 1 describe

    _____.

4. While it is not directly stated, the article suggests that
       a. The Pompeians were not very bright.
       b. More people could have escaped if they had realized the danger.
       c. Earthquakes are more dangerous than volcanoes.

5. Pompeii was buried in twelve feet of
       a. hot ash.
       b. poisonous gases.
       c. molten lava.

6. On the whole, the article tells about
       a. early attempts at predicting volcanic activity.
       b. Giuseppe Fiorelli's plan to restore Pompeii.
       c. how a volcanic eruption both destroyed and preserved a city.

7. Which statement does this article lead you to believe?
       a. Historians have no use for restorations such as Pompeii.
       b. The restoration of an ancient city is a long and expensive process.
       c. Treasure hunters took all the valuables.

8. Why did the Pompeians begin to rebuild their city after the earthquake?
       a. They didn't like living in ruins.
       b. They wanted to copy the buildings in Rome.
       c. They didn't realize the danger they were in.

9. Think about the concept for this group of articles. Which statement seems true both for the article and for the concept?
       a. It's never a good idea to ignore earthquakes.
       b. A natural disaster may preserve a treasure for future generations..
       c. Amateur excavations can produce amazing results.

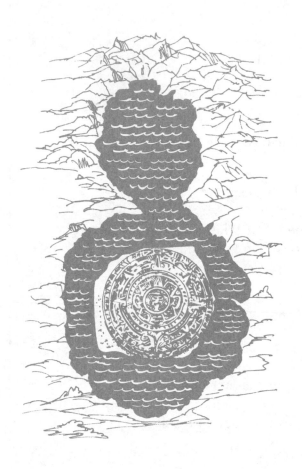

Cortez and his Spanish soldiers were the first Europeans to enter this valley. They saw the flourishing Aztec city of Tenochtitlan (tā näch′tē tlän′) rising from an island in one of the lakes. Surrounding it were green floating gardens. The Spaniards said it was as beautiful as a dream. Then the conquest began.

By 1521, when the Spaniards had conquered the fierce Aztecs, the island city was in ruins. Cortez decided to rebuild it after the pattern of European cities. Using the conquered Aztecs as slave laborers, Cortez built the new city, now Mexico City, in just four years.

"But a generation had scarcely passed after the Conquest before a sad change came over these scenes so beautiful," writes one historian. The broad, shining lakes began to dry up.

Modern historians believe that Cortez began the destruction of the valley's lakes when he ordered the city rebuilt. A great deal of charcoal was needed to burn the limestone from which cement and mortar were made. Wood was needed to finish the interiors of the buildings.

The mountainside forests were destroyed to provide the charcoal and wood. Once the slopes were bare, rainfall no longer seeped slowly into the earth to feed the springs that filled the valley's lakes. Instead, rainfall poured off the mountainsides and caused periodic flooding of the valley. To protect the city from floods, later rulers made a cut through the mountains so that the water drained away into another valley. Mexico City, once an island, had become a city on a dry plain.

Mexico's Lost Lakes

The heart of Mexico is a high, oval valley surrounded by mountains. Once, forests blanketed the mountainsides, and broad, shining lakes covered nearly all the valley floor. Now, the mountains are bare and scarred with erosion, and much of the valley floor is dry and dusty.

1. Mexico City was once an
   - a. atoll.
   - b. archipelago.
   - c. island.
   - d. eyesore.

2. The word in paragraph 5 that means *a material used to hold stones or bricks together* is _____.

3. The words "to feed the springs that filled the valley's lakes" in the last paragraph describe the _____.

4. While it is not directly stated, the article suggests that
   - a. the Aztecs didn't begin to flourish until Cortez came.
   - b. the Spaniards destroyed a civilization as well as a city.
   - c. the Spaniards brought a fine civilization to the Aztecs.

5. Mountainside forests were destroyed to provide
   - a. charcoal and wood.
   - b. rainfall and clay.
   - c. chariots and wool.

6. On the whole, the article tells about
   - a. Mexico City before and after the Spaniards came.
   - b. Mexico as it looked when it was a European city.
   - c. modern historians who write about Mexico City.

7. Which statement does this article lead you to believe?
   - a. Keeping nature's balance is not important anymore.
   - b. People thought nature's resources would last forever.
   - c. New forests always automatically replace old ones.

8. Why did later rulers cut through the mountains?
   - a. They wanted to fill the city with rainwater.
   - b. They wanted to protect the city from floods.
   - c. They wanted the valleys to flood regularly.

9. Think about the concept for this group of articles. Which statement seems true both for the article and for the concept?
   - a. Rainfall is needed only in mountain areas now.
   - b. Too many lakes spoil the appearance of the land.
   - c. Cortez believed he was building a better city.

Fighting Fog

To airlines and airport operators, fog is an enemy. When the white, misty blanket hides runways, airplanes cannot take off or land. Changes in flight schedules cost the airlines several million dollars each year.

Fog is a concentration of tiny water droplets suspended in the air. It most often occurs when warm, moist air is suddenly cooled. To clear the air of fog, it is necessary to evaporate the droplets or cause them to join together and fall as rain or snow.

In 1968, a new fog-sweeping machine was tested for dissipating the most common kind of fog, which occurs at temperatures above freezing. The machine consisted of a 100-foot-long plastic tube mounted on a mobile blower. As the machine moved across the airport, chemicals were blown through the tube and up into the fog. One of the chemicals reduced the surface tension on the water droplets so that they would join together more easily. Another chemical gave an electrical charge to the droplets, so that they attracted each other and fell as rain.

Cold fog, which occurs at temperatures below freezing, causes only a small percentage of airport shutdowns. Cold fog is fairly easy to eliminate. For quite a few years, airports have used cloud-seeding methods to dissipate cold fog. An airplane drops crystals of dry ice into the fog. Soon, snow falls and the air clears.

In the 1990s, another kind of weapon against fog was developed. Pilots who are flying through fog fire a pulse of laser light toward the runway. The light that would normally be reflected by the fog is screened out by a sensor. When the laser pulse returns, the sensor opens briefly to admit only the light reflected from the runway, thus enabling the laser to "see" the runway through the fog.

These new "weather weapons" are helping to win the war against fog.

1. Fog occurs when
   - a. cooler air is suddenly warmed.
   - c. rain and snow meet.
   - b. warm air is suddenly cooled.
   - d. air is polluted.

2. The word in paragraph 3 that means *separating* or *scattering in several directions* is _____.

3. The words "a 100-foot-long plastic tube mounted on a mobile blower" in paragraph 3 describe the _____.

4. While it is not directly stated, the article suggests that
   - a. fog can be dangerous.
   - b. fog is not important.
   - c. fog can always be cleared.

5. To dissipate fog, some airports have used
   - a. tiny water droplets.
   - b. cloud-seeding methods.
   - c. snow and ice cubes.

6. On the whole, the article tells about
   - a. the temperature needed to make a cold fog appear.
   - b. the benefits of using lasers to see through fog.
   - c. different methods used over the years to fight fog at airports.

7. Which statement does this article lead you to believe?
   - a. Some methods of dealing with fog have already been successful.
   - b. Congress is thinking of passing a law against using lasers in airplanes.
   - c. The only successful way to clear fog is by cloud-seeding.

8. Why can't airplanes land or take off when it is foggy?
   - a. Fog forms crystals of dry ice on the airplanes.
   - b. They have to wait for helicopters in fog layers.
   - c. The white, misty blanket hides the runways.

9. Think about the concept for this group of articles. Which statement seems true both for the article and for the concept?
   - a. Someday people plan to be able to control fog completely.
   - b. People should not hope to control fog completely.
   - c. There are too many "weather weapons" being used.

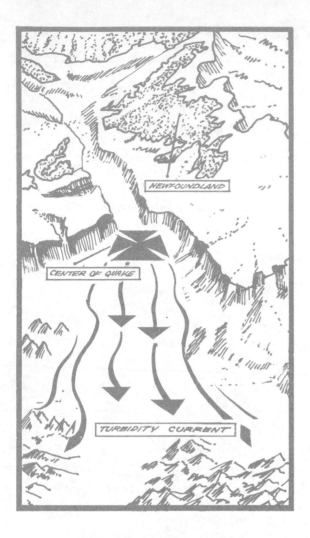

Center of Quake

Newfoundland

Turbidity Current

An Undersea Mystery

Turbidity currents are like angry, muddy rivers that flow under the surface of the sea. Until recently, scientists were not sure such currents existed. In 1929, an underwater earthquake south of Newfoundland helped scientists learn about turbidity currents.

The earthquake was centered below the continental slope. This slope marks the edge of the more gently-sloping continental shelf. It is the steep drop-off to the bottom of the sea. The quake occurred in an area crossed by many transatlantic telegraph cables lying on the ocean floor.

At the time of the quake, six of the nearest cables stopped transmitting messages. These cables were broken by the earthquake. Hours later, three other cables, which lay further south, stopped transmitting messages. No one knew what broke them. Cables a similar distance to the north were not affected.

Like detectives trying to solve a mysterious crime, scientists studied the clues. Eventually, they became convinced that the earthquake had created a turbidity current that had flowed more than 600 miles down the continental slope to break the three southernmost cables.

The earthquake had stirred up mud on the continental slope, creating a huge mass of muddy water much heavier than the water around it. Responding to gravity, the muddy water had flowed down the steep slope. As it moved, the turbidity current picked up speed and sediment. Because the scientists knew at what times the different cables had stopped transmitting, they were able to estimate how fast the current had flowed. The current had broken the last cable thirteen hours after the earthquake.

Today, scientists believe that turbidity currents help create the steep-sided submarine canyons that cut into the continental slope. Just as a river deepens a valley on land, a turbidity current can scour out a canyon under the sea.

The 1929 earthquake interrupted transatlantic telegraph service. But it added much to our knowledge of the mysterious forces of the sea.

1. In 1929, an underwater earthquake took place
    a. north of Nova Scotia.   c. west of New Mexico.
    b. south of Newfoundland.   d. east of Norway.

2. The word in paragraph 4 that means *secret, unknown, or unexplainable* is

    _____ .

3. The words "angry, muddy rivers that flow under the surface of the sea" in

    paragraph 1 describe _____ _____ .

4. While it is not directly stated, the article suggests that
    a. scientists can keep track of underwater earthquakes.
    b. it is impossible to tell when earthquakes take place.
    c. earthquakes cause damage only when they are on the surface.

5. A turbidity current can scour out a canyon
    a. through a hill.
    b. in a mountain.
    c. under the sea.

6. On the whole, the article tells about
    a. the outer limit of the gently-sloping continental shelf.
    b. muddy waters that break cables every thirteen hours.
    c. an earthquake that added to our knowledge of the sea.

7. Which statement does this article lead you to believe?
    a. We have no idea what the ocean floor is like.
    b. The ocean floor may have many features like those on the continents.
    c. The entire ocean floor is smooth and flat.

8. Why did the muddy water flow down the slope?
    a. It was responding to gravity.
    b. It had no place else to go.
    c. It was trying to get to the cables.

9. Think about the concept for this group of articles. Which statement seems true
    both for the article and for the concept?
    a. The only harm earthquakes can cause is broken cables.
    b. Violence in nature can sometimes have helpful side-effects.
    c. Nothing good can ever come from turbidity currents.

The first modern computers were built in the 1930s. They were not electric, as are today's computers. These first modern computers were mechanical monsters that filled huge rooms. A few years later, the bulky gears and shafts were replaced with electrical switches, telephone relays, and vacuum tubes. In the 1950s, transistors replaced the vacuum tubes. Transistors do the same work as vacuum tubes but are much smaller and lighter.

In the 1960s, even smaller electronic parts called chips came into use. Chips as small as a fingernail replaced the transistors and much of the wiring in computers. Their small size meant smaller computers. Some computers are small enough to be held in your hand. Such computers are used in everything from cellular phones to spacecraft, where small size and light weight are vital.

The same developments that reduced the computer's size and weight also increased its speed. For 30 years, computer chips were made from aluminum on a base of silicon. However, aluminum is not able to conduct electricity very fast. Copper is a better conductor of electricity, but copper did not work well with silicon. For years, scientists tried to find a way to make computers faster. Finally in 1997, they discovered how to make a smaller, faster, and more powerful chip. They did this by insulating, or covering, the copper so that it doesn't touch the silicon.

These new chips enable computers to run at speeds as fast as one gigahertz, or more than three times faster than the fastest previous computers. By the time you read this page, computer chips will be even faster!

The Speed of Electronic Thought

Computers are not only changing the world we live in—computers themselves are changing. They are becoming lighter, faster, and smaller.

86

1.   The new computer chips are made of
     a.   aluminum on silicon.   c.   copper on silicon.
     b.   transistors.   d.   vacuum tubes.

2.   The word in paragraph 4 that means *allow to pass through* is

     _____.

3.   The words "small enough to be held in your hand" in paragraph 3 describe
     some of the newest _____.

4.   While it is not directly stated, the article suggests that
     a.   small-size, lightweight computers are not allowed on spacecraft.
     b.   the computers we have now are perfect and do not need to be better.
     c.   computers of the future will be superior to those we have now.

5.   Smaller electronic parts came into use in the
     a.   1680s.
     b.   1960s.
     c.   1890s.

6.   On the whole, the article tells about
     a.   mathematicians and what they believe.
     b.   the first electronic computer ever built.
     c.   important developments in modern computers.

7.   Which statement does this article lead you to believe?
     a.   The increase in speed has made new problems for computers.
     b.   Computers take too long to do their calculations.
     c.   A computer can calculate faster than a person can.

8.   How did chips improve computers?
     a.   They allowed computers to become smaller.
     b.   They were mechanical.
     c.   They made electrical switches possible.

9.   Think about the concept for this group of articles. Which statement seems true
     both for the article and for the concept?
     a.   Vacuum tubes have replaced electricity and telephones.
     b.   People will continue to try to improve our computers.
     c.   Plans that reduced the speed of computers failed.

A Country in Transition

For years, the Republic of South Africa was a nation in trouble. Located at the southern tip of the continent, South Africa is the most industrialized country in Africa. It has large deposits of gold and diamonds, a good climate, and great natural beauty. But it has also been the scene of terrible racial violence. This violence was a result of the official government policy of racial segregation called apartheid, the Afrikaans word for "apartness."

Apartheid became the law of the land when the all-white minority National Party took control in 1948. This government said the new laws were necessary to avoid civil war among groups of blacks who hated each other. In addition to enforcing strict racial segregation, apartheid denied the right to vote, own land, travel, or to work without a permit to nonwhites. Nonwhites make up the majority of the population.

Opposition to the government's policies grew. The African National Congress (ANC), a black organization, led the opposition until it was outlawed in 1961. Its leader, Nelson Mandela, was sentenced to life imprisonment. These incidents aroused the rest of the world against apartheid, and many nations began to impose trade sanctions against South Africa.

Bowing to international and internal pressure, the government began to take back some of its apartheid laws in the 1970s and 1980s. Then in 1989, F. Willem de Klerk was elected president. De Klerk realized that minority rule would have to end.

1990 was an important year for South Africa. In February, de Klerk released Mandela from prison, and the government lifted the ban on black political organizations, such as the ANC. In May, the white minority government began to hold formal discussions with Mandela and the ANC. These two groups began to plan a new constitution.

In 1994, South Africa held its first election that was open to citizens of all races. Mandela was elected president. Disagreement, sometimes violent, among some South Africans still exists, but with the ending of apartheid, all citizens will have a say in helping to solve the country's problems.

FIND THE ANSWERS

1. The apartheid laws of South Africa enforced
   a. the right to vote.
   b. strict racial segregation.
   c. international trade sanctions.
   d. the African National Congress.

2. The word in paragraph 3 that means *penalties* is _____.

3. The words "who make up the majority of the population" in paragraph 2 refer to _____.

4. While it is not directly stated, the article suggests that
   a. most South Africans benefited from apartheid.
   b. apartheid was destroying South Africa.
   c. international trade sanctions never work.

5. Nelson Mandela was the leader of
   a. the National Party.
   b. the Willem de Klerk re-election campaign.
   c. the African National Congress.

6. On the whole, the article tells about
   a. the history of a failed government policy in South Africa.
   b. the political failure of the African National Congress.
   c. a new constitution for South Africa.

7. Which statement does this article lead you to believe?
   a. Most South Africans do not care about government.
   b. Government by a minority is unfair.
   c. Different races will never be able to live peacefully in South Africa.

8. Why did the government begin to repeal apartheid laws?
   a. Apartheid had served its purpose and was no longer necessary.
   b. The government was under pressure from other countries.
   c. It wanted to create better apartheid laws.

9. Think about the concept for this group of articles. Which statement seems true both for the article and for the concept?
   a. South Africans will soon be able to put apartheid behind them.
   b. South Africa needs to cooperate more with neighboring countries.
   c. South Africa will fare better with a majority government.

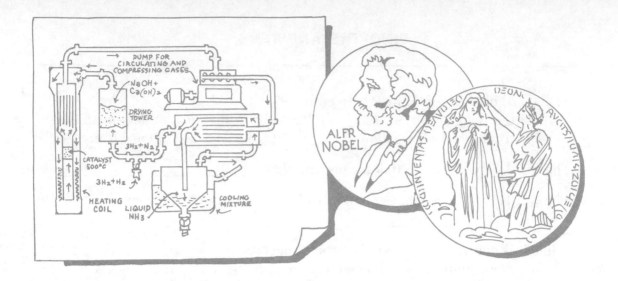

A Chemist Finds a Way

Except for coal, Germany has never had the great supplies of raw materials that an industrial nation needs. Yet Germany has many industries. Some of them were made possible by its scientists. These scientists found ways to produce raw materials Germany needed from the few raw materials that Germany had.

Until the beginning of World War I, Germany imported large amounts of nitrogen compounds from Chile. Some nitrogen compounds occur naturally in the soil. Germany used these imported nitrogen compounds to produce chemicals such as ammonia, a necessary ingredient in explosives and fertilizers.

When World War I began in 1914, British ships moved quickly to blockade Germany's seaports. Because of the blockade, Germany could no longer import nitrogen compounds from South America, just at a time when they were needed more than ever before. To carry on the war, the German army had to have ammonia to make its explosives. To produce enough food for the people to eat, German farmers had to have fertilizers.

In 1914, the German chemist Fritz Haber offered his services to his government. He knew how important nitrogen compounds were to the war effort. Fritz Haber had already planned and developed new ways to produce them. From his thinking came a new process for producing ammonia by mixing nitrogen from air with hydrogen from water. A fellow scientist, Carl Bosch, adapted the process for industrial use. The synthetic ammonia was used to make the explosives and fertilizers that Germany needed to carry on the war.

Although the Haber-Bosch process was a response to a wartime need, it has proved widely useful in peacetime. For his work, Fritz Haber received the 1918 Nobel Prize in chemistry. The world's great industries owe much to the scientists who plan ways to make materials people need from the raw materials at hand.

1. One of Germany's few raw materials has been
   a. bronze.   c. iron.
   b. copper.   d. coal.

2. The word in paragraph 4 that means changed or made to fit some thing else
   is _____.

3. The words "who plan ways to make materials people need" in the last paragraph describe _____.

4. While it is not directly stated, the article suggests that
   a. all of Germany's scientists refused to help their country.
   b. most governments find their scientists cannot help them.
   c. scientists are of great importance to their governments.

5. To carry on the war, the German army had to have
   a. ammonia.
   b. azaleas.
   c. Arizona.

6. On the whole, the article tells about
   a. German farmers who wanted fertilizers.
   b. the creation of new products in wartime.
   c. the 1918 Nobel Prize given to artists.

7. Which statement does this article lead you to believe?
   a. A scientific process can apply to many fields.
   b. All scientists must now be chemists only.
   c. South American scientists have gone to Germany.

8. Why wouldn't Germany import nitrogen compounds?
   a. It preferred to import hydrogen instead.
   b. Its ports were blockaded by England.
   c. South America ran out of the compounds.

9. Think about the concept for this group of articles. Which statement seems true
   both for the article and for the concept?
   a. A war emergency is the only thing that creates new ideas.
   b. Anything planned during an emergency will always fail.
   c. Good plans sometimes are the result of emergencies.

A Lucky Accident

In the early 1800s, people were fascinated by the curious substance made from the sap of tropical American trees. The substance was pure rubber. From it, balls were made for children's play, and erasers for rubbing out pencil marks. Pure rubber was used to make boots and waterproof cloth for raincoats, but these articles often hardened or melted in the changeable climate of North America.

Pure rubber melts when it is heated, and turns hard and brittle when it is chilled. Before rubber could be used for most purposes, it had to be changed in a way that would make it tougher and more resistant to extremes of temperature.

A young hardware merchant from Connecticut was one of the persons interested in the stretchy, bouncy substance. His name was Charles Goodyear. Convinced that pure rubber had great possibilities, he neglected his business to experiment with it. His business failed, and he was jailed for debt. Once he even sold his children's schoolbooks to get money to carry on his experiments.

Yet Goodyear succeeded where others experimenting with rubber failed. He tried mixing pure rubber with sulfur.

Accidently, he dropped some of this mixture on a hot stove. To his surprise, this rubber did not melt when hot. When it was cooled, it was still stretchy. He nailed it to the outside of a doorframe and left it overnight, but the frost did not make it hard and brittle.

Goodyear named his process of heating rubber and sulfur "vulcanization," after Vulcan, the Roman god of fire. Vulcanized rubber made possible bicycle tires, pulley belts, and rubber parts for machinery. Later, automobile tires and a thousand other useful articles were manufactured from Charles Goodyear's "accident": vulcanized rubber.

FIND THE ANSWERS

1. Goodyear tried mixing pure rubber with
   - a. plasma.
   - b. topsoil.
   - c. crystals.
   - d. sulfur.

2. The word in paragraph 2 that means *easily broken* is _____.

3. The words "from the sap of tropical American trees" in paragraph 1 describe the curious _____.

4. While it is not directly stated, the article suggests that
   - a. vulcanized rubber is used in many industries.
   - b. useful articles cannot be made from rubber.
   - c. vulcanized rubber comes from American trees.

5. "Vulcanization" was named for Vulcan,
   - a. the Trojan god of war.
   - b. the Roman god of fire.
   - c. the Greek god of sulfur.

6. On the whole, the article tells about
   - a. products made from pure rubber.
   - b. the changeable climate of North America.
   - c. Goodyear's discovery of vulcanized rubber.

7. Which statement does this article lead you to believe?
   - a. Vulcanized rubber is the only product discovered by accident.
   - b. When experiments fail, inventors should stop experimenting.
   - c. Many new products were created with the use of vulcanized rubber.

8. What is one reason vulcanized rubber is better than pure rubber?
   - a. Vulcanized rubber is not affected by climate.
   - b. Boots and erasers cannot be made from pure rubber.
   - c. Vulcanized rubber is made from pure sulfur.

9. Think about the concept for this group of articles. Which statement seems true both for the article and for the concept?
   - a. An important discovery can be made by accident.
   - b. Goodyear succeeded because his business failed.
   - c. An invention can never come about by chance.

Artists of the North

Carving was once the Inuits' way of making the tools and utensils they needed to live. From ivory, bone, and driftwood they carved knife handles, harpoons, and buttons. From soapstone they carved oil lamps and cooking pots.

Today, the Inuit buy factory-made tools and utensils instead of carving them. But they continue to carve as a means of artistic expression and as a way to earn money. Inuit carvings are shown in museums and art galleries, and they are sold in many city gift shops.

The popularity of Inuit carving was sparked by James Houston, an artist who made a painting trip to Northern Canada in 1948. Visiting Port Harrison on Hudson Bay, he learned how a dwindling supply of game made it difficult for the native people to earn a living by fur trapping. Houston admired some small soapstone statues carved by the Port Harrison Inuit. He recognized their natural talent as artists. They needed only encouragement and help in marketing their work.

Much of the art Houston saw portrays Arctic birds and animals and parka-clad men and women working at traditional tasks. The best pieces express Inuit pride in the old way of life, the way of the hunter.

In Montreal and other Canadian cities, Houston showed samples of Inuit carving. He also discussed his plan for helping the Inuit. Backed by private citizens and later by the Canadian government, he made many trips to settlements in the far north. There, he urged more people to take up carving and other art forms. Houston

bought the pieces and shipped them south to be sold.

Thanks to the encouragement and help of James Houston, Inuit art is sold and admired all over the world. Through their art, these people have found new ways of earning a good living.

1. Houston admired some small soapstone statues carved by the
   a. Port Harrison Inuit.   c. Montreal Inuit.
   b. Fort Morrison Indians.   d. Antarctic Indians.

2. The word in paragraph 4 that means *pictures* or *represents as in a drawing* is
   _____.

3. The words "an artist who made a painting trip to Northern Canada" in paragraph 3 describe _____ _____.

4. While it is not directly stated, the article suggests that
   a. native people use materials at hand in their art.
   b. native people are not interested in art forms.
   c. carvings and statues are not good art expressions.

5. Houston showed samples of the carving in
   a. Madison.
   b. Montreal.
   c. Montauk.

6. On the whole, the article tells about
   a. one artist's efforts to encourage Inuit art.
   b. factory-made tools and utensils sold to the Inuit.
   c. painting trips made to Northern Canada by Houston.

7. Which statement does this article lead you to believe?
   a. People around the world like Inuit art.
   b. Inuit art is sold only in parts of Canada now.
   c. The best pieces of Inuit art portray Houston.

8. Why was it difficult for the Inuit to earn a living by fur trapping?
   a. Fur trapping is too hard for the Inuit.
   b. The Inuit were too lazy to hunt.
   c. The supply of game was dwindling.

9. Think about the concept for this group of articles. Which statement seems true both for the article and for the concept?
   a. Earning money through art was planned by an interested outsider.
   b. The Inuit do not need to earn money because they have great talent.
   c. The Inuit continue to earn money by making utensils for factories.

A New Craft for the Navaho

The Navaho Indians of Arizona and New Mexico are well known for their work with silver. They make silver bracelets and belt buckles stamped with intricate patterns of wavy lines, crescent moons, and arrowheads. They make silver rings set with turquoise stones. Many people proudly wear Navaho jewelry. Navaho silverwork is often shown in museums and art galleries.

Most people are surprised to learn that silversmithing is not an ancient art of the Navaho. It is likely that they did not learn much about working with silver until about 1869. Before that time, the Navaho obtained most of their silver jewelry from Mexican villages south of the border.

The Mexicans were skilled silversmiths, but the Navaho did not have much chance to learn the craft from them because the two peoples were enemies. The Navaho repeatedly raided Mexican villages.

This border warfare between Navaho and Mexicans made trouble for the United States government. Finally Colonel Kit Carson was sent with United States Army troops to enforce a peace. When other measures failed, the Navaho were confined at Fort Sumner for about four years.

During 1867 and 1868, the Navaho were freed. They returned to their old territory, where they were given new livestock by the United States government. There were no more raids across the border. Instead, Navahos peacefully watched Mexican silversmiths at work and learned from them. Soon the Navaho were melting down silver coins and reshaping the metal into ornaments. They began to earn money by selling silver jewelry to other tribes and to tourists who visited the Navaho reservation.

The peace that followed the border warfare brought the Navaho an unexpected benefit. It gave them a chance to learn a new and profitable craft—a craft at which they became experts.

1. The Mexicans were skilled
   a. silversmiths.
   b. locksmiths.
   c. blacksmiths.
   d. goldsmiths.

2. The word in paragraph 1 that means *complicated* is _____.

3. The words "who visited the Navaho reservation" in paragraph 5 describe _____.

4. While it is not directly stated, the article suggests that
   a. neighbors always war with each other.
   b. the effort that goes into warfare can be put to better use.
   c. warfare often results in people learning from one another.

5. During 1867 and 1868, the Navaho were
   a. found.
   b. chained.
   c. freed.

6. On the whole, the article tells about
   a. the livestock given to all the Navaho.
   b. Mexicans who visited Navaho reservations.
   c. a craft one people learned from another.

7. Which statement does this article lead you to believe?
   a. Tourists are glad to buy Navaho jewelry.
   b. Navaho jewelry is made mostly by tourists.
   c. Tourists cannot buy any Navaho jewelry.

8. Why did the United States government send troops?
   a. The troops heard the Mexicans had silver.
   b. The troops wanted to recruit the Navaho.
   c. The troops were sent to enforce a peace.

9. Think about the concept for this group of articles. Which statement seems true both for the article and for the concept?
   a. Art must be planned to be successful.
   b. New art forms grow in unexpected ways.
   c. Only modern people accept new art forms.

The Sun Sisters

Who lives in the sun? A fire dragon? A god of fire? Some say that it is really a golden raven. And that is why the Chinese make a special sign for the sun —a bird in a circle. But why can't you look into the sun? You can look at the moon and see shapes and faces, but the sun is different.

The Chinese tell a tale about the sun. It goes like this.

Long, long ago, a young man lived in the sun. He had two young sisters who lived in the moon. It is said of these two sisters that they were quite beautiful. People said that they were like two blossoms in a garden.

People told of their beauty, which was like the beauty of nature. The sisters were slender as the bamboo. They were as graceful as willow branches. Their faces were shaped like the oval seeds of the melon. Their hair was like the black of night, and around their dark eyes were circles as white as the snow.

The beauty of the sisters was known throughout the land. But they were not only beautiful. They were as clever as they were beautiful. They spent their days stitching with embroidery needles.

They were very skilled. They covered their silken robes with the finest stitches. They covered their delicate slippers with stitches just as delicate. They could make flowers lovelier than any in the garden.

They stitched dragons, birds, and butterflies with thousands of fine, tiny stitches. Their robes looked like the paintings of the greatest painters.

All night, the sisters stitched by the light of the moon. The skill of these sisters spread throughout the land. People heard of the beauty of their robes made with the finest of stitches. On clear nights, people gathered in their gardens. They strained their eyes to see these wonderful sisters in the moon. They climbed the hills and mountains to look up at the moon. They wanted to catch a glimpse of these young women.

From their high palace, the sisters watched. And they were not at all pleased. At that time, it was the custom that young maidens were not to be stared at, especially by young men.

As the sisters watched the people below, they became distressed. So many people came out at night to gaze at them. What could they do? Each night as they stitched, they began to think of ways to avoid the stares. With each tiny stitch, they searched their minds. They thought of hiding, but they disliked that idea. They had done nothing wrong, why should they hide?

Finally, one of the sisters said, "I think I have the solution. We will go to our dear brother in the sun and ask him to change places with us. We will live in the sun and he will live in the moon."

"What a wonderful plan!" said her sister. "We must leave at once to visit our brother in the sun." The two sisters put on their finest robes and set off to present their plan.

As they approached the shining palace in the sun, they called out to their brother. "Oh, great and wise brother, we have had great problems."

"What can be troubling you, my sisters? You are fair and talented and you have each other for company. What can possibly be troubling you?"

One of the sisters spoke up. "It is true, my brother, we are quite lucky to have such beauty around us. We love to be with one another and we love each minute that we stitch our colorful designs. But the trouble is not with us. It is with others."

"Yes," said the other sister, afraid that they had displeased their brother. "We are happy in our home, but we are not happy with the people below. Each night, when people come out in their gardens, they stare up at us. It should not be like this. We are unhappy."

Their brother was not happy when he heard their story. He agreed that it was not proper for the people to stare. "Well, I will think of a plan," the brother offered.

"If it please you, my brother, we have spent long hours thinking of a plan of our own. We think it will work." Then the sisters told him of their plan to live in the sun.

The brother listened carefully. He began to laugh. "Now, you are really being silly," he told them. "If you are

99

bothered by people at night, what will happen by day? In the daylight, when my sunlight shines, there are many, many more people awake than at night. If you change places with me, what will you do with these thousands more eyes that will be gazing at you?"

The sisters did not mind their brother's protests. They insisted, "Oh, please, dear brother, if you will just cooperate with us, you will learn that we have a way to make our plan work. You must trust us and we will be successful."

The brother had great doubts, but he loved his sisters, and he knew that they were not foolish. At last, he agreed and made plans to change places with his sisters. He would dwell in the moon and they would take his place in the sun.

The sisters were delighted. They sang as they gathered their beautiful robes and their delicate slippers. These precious belongings were carefully packed into a shiny red chest. They placed their tiny needles in a special case. This, too, was placed most carefully into the shiny red chest.

With their precious robes packed and their precious needles safe, they quickly made their way to their new home. In no time at all, they were completely settled in their bright dwelling.

At night, the people below came out to look for the sisters. They were bewildered. What had happened to the beauties in the moon? Quickly, the word spread. If they wished to see the beauty of the sisters, they must look to the sun.

Thousands of curious eyes gazed into the daytime skies. But the sisters plan protected them. People turned away in pain. Each time the people would gaze up at them, the sisters would sting them with their tiny, sharp embroidery needles. "The sun's rays are too bright," people said. "They hurt our eyes." Try as they might, the people below could never again glimpse the two sisters.

Perhaps you, too, have tried to gaze at the sun and have felt your eyes sting as a result. Perhaps the sisters' plan is still working.   (1105 words)

III

Modern Ways of Life
Require Planned Change

In this section, you will read about many ways in which people must plan for the future. You will read about these things in the areas of history, space, biology, anthropology, economics, geography, Earth science, mathematics, engineering, and art.

Keep these questions in mind when you are reading.

1. What are some planned changes that have affected our country?

2. What are some changes that have affected us as individuals?

3. Are all planned changes necessarily good?

4. If all changes are not good, what can you do to correct the change?

5. What palnning must take place to cause changes to occur?

Look on pages 10-11 for help with words you don't understand in this section.

History at Your Fingertips

Not long ago, most historians had to be travelers. To consult written accounts of historical events, they had to travel to the places where the accounts were stored. To read rare old books and other documents, they often had to visit museums and libraries far from home.

Today, the technology available at most libraries is one of the historian's best research tools. Because of it, historians are no longer limited to the books a given library happens to have in its collection. A computerized national library network gives historians and students access to any book in the U.S.—even to books from some foreign countries. Filling out a request card is usually all it takes. People can even access the national library network from their homes via the Internet.

This system works well for fairly recent books. But what about old, rare, or extremely valuable books and other documents that cannot travel? Today, historians can also examine these documents in local libraries. Rare books, letters, old newspa-

pers, and other historical documents have been microfilmed.

Microfilming is a photographic process which copies and reduces pages of printed matter to small reels of film. Up to 5,000 book pages can be copied on one reel of microfilm. A reel takes up less storage space than a book and can be mailed with ease to libraries all across the country and around the world. To read microfilm, the user places the reel in a machine which projects a full-sized image on a screen. Thus, American students of European history can now see, on microfilm, documents dating back to the time of King Henry VII of England. And European students of American history can consult the records of the first United States Congress.

Each year, more old and rare material is transferred to microfilm. With the advances in computer technology, some of this material is also being made available on CD-ROM. Both computerized sharing among library systems and microfilming use the technology of today to save the past for the future.

1. In order to read old documents, historians once had to
    a. get permission from the U.S. Congress.   c. travel to England.
    b. travel to faraway museums and libraries.   d. use a CD-ROM.

2. The word in paragraph 2 that means *the right to make use of* is
   _____.

3. The words "one of the historian's best research tools" in paragraph 2 refer to
   _____.

4. While it is not directly stated, the article suggests that
    a. rare books and documents are to be treasured.
    b. all rare books are kept in foreign countries.
    c. most American students now own rare books.

5. To locate books that are not in the local library, the researcher uses
    a. a microfilm machine.
    b. a microwave machine.
    c. the computerized national library network.

6. On the whole, the article tells about
    a. European students of American history.
    b. documents written by King Henry VII.
    c. gaining access to books and other research materials.

7. Which statement does this article lead you to believe?
    a. Microfilm is useful in many fields.
    b. Only historians ever use library computers or microfilm.
    c. It takes a long time to obtain books from other libraries.

8. Why are rare documents transferred to microfilm?
    a. The first United States Congress ordered this done.
    b. It makes them available to more people and it protects them
       for the future.
    c. It takes less time to read smaller pages.

9. Think about the concept for this group of articles. Which statement seems
   true both for the article and for the concept?
    a. Today's historians use modern methods in research.
    b. Microfilming of documents goes back to King Henry VII.
    c. Computers will soon eliminate books entirely.

TUBMAN

DREW

WOODS

CHISHOLM

WHEATLEY

BANNEKER

MATZELIGER

African Americans in Our Past

For centuries, history textbooks used in American schools neglected the role of African Americans in shaping history. Often, textbooks mentioned only Harriet Tubman, George Washington Carver, and Booker T. Washington as important African Americans. As a result, many people do not yet know about other African Americans who contributed to our past.

Older American history books did not mention Benjamin Banneker, an important figure in colonial days. Although he was a scientist, mathematician, and writer, Benjamin Banneker is best known for his role in helping to plan the nation's capital. He was appointed by George Washington to serve on the committee that planned Washington, D.C.

Until recently, students did not learn about African-American inventors. An important inventor was Granville T. Woods, who invented the automatic air brake used on railroad trains. Another African-American inventor, Jan Matzeliger, invented a machine that combined the many separate steps of shoe manufacture. Today, a multimillion-dollar shoe company still uses his invention. Sarah B. Walker became the first self-made woman millionaire in the U.S. in 1910 when she invented a method for straightening curly hair. She gave much of her fortune away to black charities.

Historically, African Americans have also made important contributions in the field of medicine. In 1893, an African American, Dr. Daniel Hale Williams, performed the world's first successful open-heart surgery. In the 1940s, Dr. Charles Drew developed the first useful system for storing blood in blood banks. Dr. Percy Julian helped develop drugs used to treat arthritis.

Today, history textbooks are changing. Increasingly, educators, authors, and publishers are producing textbooks that recognize the role of African Americans. Americans have come to realize that the record of their history is not complete without the major contributions of African Americans.

1. Granville T. Woods invented the
   a. time machine.
   b. jet airplane.
   c. automatic air brake.
   d. automobile hand brake.

2. The word in paragraph 1 that means *paid no attention to* is

   _____.

3. The words "an important figure in colonial days" in paragraph 2 describe

   _____   _____.

4. While it is not directly stated, the article suggests that
   a. students have always been aware of the role of African Americans.
   b. history textbooks never omit any known historical facts.
   c. students have much to learn about the history of African Americans.

5. A machine invented by Jan Matzeliger is used in
   a. the drug industry.
   b. television shows.
   c. shoe manufacture.

6. On the whole, the article tells about
   a. the important role of African Americans in U.S. history.
   b. drugs that have been used to cure arthritis.
   c. the committee that helped plan the nation's capital.

7. Which statement does this article lead you to believe?
   a. The record of the African-American community is important to all Americans.
   b. There were only three important African Americans in U.S. history.
   c. The African-American community is important only today.

8. Why was Dr. Daniel Hale Williams' contribution so important?
   a. He was the first man to put blood in a bank system.
   b. He paved the way to successful open-heart surgery.
   c. He owned a multimillion-dollar shoe company.

9. Think about the concept for this group of articles. Which statement seems true both for the article and for the concept?
   a. African Americans are especially fine inventors.
   b. The contributions of African Americans have always been recognized.
   c. African Americans must be recognized for their contributions to history.

Conquering Math Anxiety

In 1989, educators in this country began to call attention to a national problem: most students leave American schools without the mathematical skills needed for jobs or for higher education. This was especially true for female and minority students. The Educational Testing Service reported that, in an international survey, American teenagers had the lowest math scores.

This situation has been defined as "innumeracy," or the inability to grasp the basic idea of mathematics. Mathematicians, teachers, and scientists were alarmed by these findings because the modern world depends upon math and science technology. They looked for the reasons for innumeracy and decided that, in addition to poor education, there are many psychological blocks to acquiring an understanding of mathematics.

Embarrassment about not knowing math can lead to fear in the classroom. Fear can lead to silence because students do not want to draw attention to their lack of knowledge. As a result, those students fall further and further behind. Low visibility in the classroom has not always been recognized as a silent call for help.

Math educators decided to try to change that. In 1990, the Mathematical Sciences Education Board called for a change in the way math is taught in the United States.

Math reform is beginning with the educators themselves. Teachers are now being trained to recognize and to help students work through "math anxiety"—the roadblocks on their way to gaining competence in mathematics. In addition, math textbooks are being updated to help students understand that math is not a sort of foreign language of numbers. Math is a tool that helps us to analyze patterns and structures, and to discover relationships.

The traditional computing skills of addition, subtraction, multiplication, and division are still being taught, of course. However, there is added emphasis on logical thinking and creative problem solving, for which there may be several equally valid solutions.

Revised math programs being created now will ensure that American students will be prepared for the twenty-first century.

1. The Educational Testing Service reported that American teenagers had
    a. the highest math scores.
    b. the lowest math scores.
    c. average math scores.
    d. above average math scores.

2. The word in paragraph 6 that means *sound* or *reasonable* is

    _____.

3. The words "the inability to grasp the basic idea of mathematics" in paragraph 2 are the definition of _____.

4. While it is not directly stated, the article suggests that
    a. methods of teaching should change from time to time.
    b. subjects should always be taught in the same way.
    c. most students found mathematics to be an exciting subject.

5. Mathematics helps us to analyze
    a. the Education Testing Service.
    b. the twenty-first century.
    c. patterns and structures.

6. On the whole, the article tells about
    a. unfair practices of the Educational Testing Service.
    b. improvements in mathematics education.
    c. the decreasing need for mathematics education.

7. Which statement does this article lead you to believe?
    a. People understood math better before 1989.
    b. Two-thirds of America's schools do not teach math.
    c. In the future, math will be taught differently.

8. Why were educators alarmed about innumeracy in the United States?
    a. The modern world depends on math and science technology.
    b. They didn't want to give up their old teaching methods.
    c. No other country had problems teaching math.

9. Think about the concept for this group of articles. Which statement seems true both for the article and for the concept?
    a. Advanced technology demands greater innumeracy.
    b. Mathematics should be taught by foreign language instructors.
    c. Math education is changing in response to technology.

Cooperation in Space

On October 4, 1957, Earth's first artificial satellite was rocketed into orbit. That satellite was the Soviet *Sputnik I*. This date marked the beginning of the Space Age and the beginning of a "space race" between Cold War enemies—the United States and the Soviet Union. One after another, these two nations launched spacecraft to orbit Earth and its moon, Venus, and Mars. They launched unmanned probes to study other planets, and space stations to orbit Earth.

On April 12, 1961, Yuri Gagarin of Russia became the first man to orbit Earth in the spacecraft *Vostok I*. On February 20, 1962, United States astronaut John Glenn orbited Earth in the spacecraft *Friendship 7*.

This race came to an end in 1972 when the United States and the Soviet Union agreed to a joint manned space mission. This mission, called the Apollo-Soyuz Test Project, took place in 1975. It consisted of a rendezvous, or meeting, between orbiting spacecraft from each nation. Despite this success, a real joint mission in space was still twenty years in the future.

As the Cold War drew to a close, the United States proposed building a large, permanent space station to orbit Earth. In 1993, the plans for this space station were modified to save time and money, *and* to make the station international. The United States, Russia, Japan, Canada, and the European Space Agency (with 14 member nations) are scheduled to participate in its design and construction. Because of its size, this space station will have to be assembled in space. As many as 50 flights may be necessary to deliver all the components. To meet this need, several countries are now working on designs for a spacecraft that will be able to take off from Earth without the booster rockets currently needed, maneuver in space, and return to Earth—all under its own power.

Meanwhile, other international efforts in space are already taking place. In 1995, the United States space shuttle *Atlantis* docked with the Russian space station *Mir*, which means "peace." Aboard *Mir*, Americans and Russians trained and tested equipment that will be used on the International Space Station. It may well be that cooperation in space will provide a model for cooperation here on Earth.

FIND THE ANSWERS

1. The first artificial satellite, *Sputnik I*, was launched by
   a. the United States.
   b. the Soviet Union.
   c. the Apollo-Soyuz Test Project.
   d. the European Space Agency.

2. The word in paragraph 4 that means *to move carefully* is

   _____.

3. The words "first man to orbit Earth" in paragraph 2 describe

   _____ _____.

4. While it is not directly stated, the article suggests that
   a. scientists of many nations want to work together.
   b. the Cold War was hard on scientists.
   c. scientists will never learn to pool their knowledge.

5. Engineers are designing a spacecraft that will be able to take off without
   a. astronauts.
   b. replacement parts.
   c. booster rockets.

6. On the whole, the article tells about
   a. using satellites to win wars.
   b. cooperation between nations on space projects.
   c. the race to build space stations.

7. Which statement does this article lead you to believe?
   a. Cooperation in space is necessary to avoid alien attack.
   b. Cooperation in space will help many nations.
   c. Cooperation in space is doomed to failure.

8. Why must the International space station be assembled in space?
   a. It will be too large for a Space Shuttle to carry it into orbit.
   b. It would be too dangerous to assemble it on Earth.
   c. Its construction will provide practice for later space missions.

9. Think about the concept for this group of articles. Which statement seems true both for the article and for the concept?
   a. Nations will never share scientific information with each other.
   b. Modern nations must plan to work together for the good of all.
   c. International security requires all nations to explore space independently.

Farm-Fresh Fish

The salmon is one of our most valuable fish. It offers us food, sport, and profit. Every year commercial fishing results in a harvest of over a billion pounds of salmon from the sea. Hundreds of thousands of salmon are caught each year by eager sports fishers.

In autumn, the rivers of the northwestern United States come alive with salmon. They have left the ocean on their yearly run upriver to spawn. Yet today, there are far fewer salmon in the Northwest and elsewhere than ever before, because the salmon population suffers from many perils of the modern age.

Water pollution has killed many salmon by robbing them of oxygen. Overfishing has further decreased their numbers. Dams are another danger, because they block migration paths. Fish ladders, made up of stepped pools, have been built so that salmon can swim safely over the dams. But young salmon swimming to the ocean have trouble finding the ladders. Often they fall to their deaths over the dam or are killed in giant hydroelectric turbines.

To replenish the salmon supply, conservationists have turned to fish farming, or aquaculture. Farm-raised salmon are Atlantic salmon, and most are raised in the United States, Canada, Scotland, and Norway. In a typical salmon farm, the fish remain in hatcheries until they are eight inches in length. Then they are transferred to large net cages along the coast. There they are fed a diet of fishmeal until they reach market size of eight pounds, in about 18 months.

Aquaculture is one of the world's fastest growing food industries. It is replacing commercial fishing in many locales, and reducing the price of salmon to about a third of its earlier price. An added benefit is that aquaculture is allowing the wild salmon population to recover. An estimated quarter of a million more salmon returned to their home rivers to spawn each year in the mid-1990s.

1. Once salmon have been transferred to large cages, they reach market size in about
   - a. 18 months.
   - b. 8 months.
   - c. 3 years.
   - d. 18 weeks.

2. The word in paragraph 5 that means *to lay eggs* is _____.

3. The words "come alive with salmon" in paragraph 2 refer to _____.

4. While it is not directly stated, the article suggests that
   - a. salmon are found only in fresh waters.
   - b. there is no salmon fishing in the United States.
   - c. many people enjoy eating salmon.

5. Water pollution robs salmon of
   - a. plants.
   - b. ladders.
   - c. oxygen.

6. On the whole, the article tells about
   - a. stepped pools in some dams.
   - b. conserving a valuable fish.
   - c. giant hydroelectric turbines.

7. Which statement does the article lead you to believe?
   - a. Salmon cannot spawn in the ocean.
   - b. There are giants in most turbines.
   - c. Dams are built of migration blocks.

8. Why are young salmon removed from hatcheries?
   - a. Conservationists hope to reduce the number of salmon.
   - b. They are transferred to large cages so that they can grow.
   - c. They prefer fishmeal to hatchery food.

9. Think about the concept for this group of articles. Which statement seems true both for the article and for the concept?
   - a. Conservationists have many plans to preserve our animal life.
   - b. Conservationists are people who build ladders in pools.
   - c. Conservationists are only interested in salmon as food.

Pollution Is Everybody's Business

We human beings live in a natural environment, just as plants and animals do. But there is a difference: we have changed the environment to suit our needs. In past centuries, people cut down forests and plowed up prairies. We dammed up some rivers and dug new courses for others. We hunted some animals into extinction and increased the numbers of others.

Since the beginning of the Industrial Age, we have changed the environment more rapidly than ever before. Cities, factories, and vehicles produce millions of tons of poisonous wastes, which have been carelessly released into streams, lakes, oceans, and into the air.

Into the streams, lakes, and oceans go raw sewage from cities and poisonous chemicals from factories. Into the air go smoke, factory fumes, and poisonous gases from car and truck exhausts. Millions of fish, birds, land animals, and plants have already been killed by air and water pollution. Pollution contributes to cancer, heart disease, and respiratory diseases in human beings.

The United States needed laws requiring cities and factories to purify their waste products before dumping them into streams and lakes. Industry needed ways to purify gases before releasing them into the atmosphere.

In 1966, Congress voted 3 1/2 billion dollars to help American cities build new and better sewage disposal plants. A 1968 law required all new cars to have devices that reduce exhaust fumes. In 1970, Congress passed the Clean Air Act, which gave the Environmental Protection Agency the power to set antipollution standards. Then in 1990, Congress made the Clean Air Act even tougher, targeting smog, acid rain, ozone, lead, and cancer-causing agents in the air.

We are realizing that we must take better care of our environment. Otherwise, one day there may be no fresh air to breathe and no fresh water to drink.

1. Human beings have changed their environment rapidly since the
    a. Ice Age.
    c. Pennsylvanian Age.
    b. Bronze Age.
    d. Industrial Age.

2. The word in paragraph 1 that means *no longer existing* is

    _____.

3. The words "into streams, lakes, and into the air" in paragraph 2 refer to

    _____.

4. While it is not directly stated, the article suggests that
    a. animals should be hunted until they are extinct.
    b. some animals have disappeared from Earth forever.
    c. hunters help increase the number of wild animals.

5. A new law required new autos to have devices that reduced
    a. respiration.
    b. exhaust fumes.
    c. sand dunes.

6. On the whole, the article tells about
    a. the effects of pollution on our environment.
    b. animals who live in an artificial environment.
    c. the proper way to introduce poisonous gases.

7. Which statement does this article lead you to believe?
    a. People have always used our natural resources wisely.
    b. Without laws, people are careless of the environment.
    c. People do not need fresh air to breathe or fresh water to drink.

8. Why did Congress change the Clean Air Act in 1990?
    a. There was not enough air pollution to go around.
    b. The original Clean Air Act was a failure.
    c. Congress wanted to make the Clean Air Act tougher.

9. Think about the concept for this group of articles. Which statement seems
    true both for the article and for the concept?
    a. Proper planning may still save our natural environment.
    b. We can rely on Congress to do our thinking for us.
    c. People cannot get cancer without the help of air pollution.

Cultures in Conflict

In West Africa in 1900, a British governor's demand that an Ashanti tribe surrender a golden stool started a small war. The governor, believing the stool to be a throne, thought that possessing it would establish his authority over the tribe.

The stool, however, was no mere throne; it was a sacred relic that contained the spirit of the tribe. It was so sacred that not even the Ashanti chief would sit upon it. Rather than surrender the stool, the tribe hid it. British soldiers were ordered in, and many people were killed. This war and its tragic consequences were avoidable.

The science of anthropology—the study of people, how they live, and their customs and beliefs—began in the mid 1800s. At that time, anthropologists believed that human culture evolved from lower to higher forms of society and technology. However, by the time of the governor's blunder, those early beliefs had given way to the study and documentation of differences between cultures. Had the governor consulted an anthropologist, he would have had a much better chance of understanding the real meaning of the stool, and many lives could have been saved.

Modern anthropologists study every level of society. One of their main goals is to uncover universal patterns of human behavior. To avoid mistakes like that made by the unfortunate British governor, people routinely seek the advice of anthropologists.

For example, the Peace Corps sends volunteers around the world to help people in unindustrialized countries learn how to improve their lives. This was a noble idea. Yet in the early years of the Peace Corps, most volunteers were inexperienced, and few bothered to learn the language of their assigned country prior to their arrival there. Today, thanks to anthropology, the Peace Corps has changed. Its volunteers are more experienced. They have some basic language training, and they have learned how to understand and show respect for the customs and beliefs of emerging nations.

1. The governor could have avoided war by consulting an
   a. anthropologist.   c. anarchist.
   b. astrophysicist.   d. allergist.

2. The word in paragraph 2 that means *holy* is _____.

3. The word "inexperienced" in paragraph 5 describes_____.

4. While it is not directly stated, the article suggests that
   a. symbols have different meanings for different people.
   b. a throne is the only kind of symbol people respect.
   c. the governor understood the true meaning of the symbol.

5. Anthropologists today are helping young men and women of the
   a. Marine Corps.
   b. Peace Corps.
   c. Apple Cores.

6. On the whole, the article tells about
   a. the need to understand the customs and beliefs of different societies.
   b. the importance of an Ashanti chief in the governor's society.
   c. the need to advance the confusion of anthropologists in our society.

7. Which statement does the article lead you to believe?
   a. The transition to modern times is very difficult for some people.
   b. Emerging nations have no problems fitting into the modern world.
   c. Tribe members who want to be modern must hide their sacred relics.

8. Why did the governor want the golden stool of the Ashanti tribe?
   a. He thought it would help him show his authority over the tribe.
   b. He thought the golden stool did not belong to these tribe members.
   c. He thought the stool was a sacred relic belonging to Europeans.

9. Think about the concept for this group of articles. Which statement seems true both for the article and for the concept?
   a. No one can ever learn the customs and beliefs of other nations.
   b. It is important to understand the customs only of your own country.
   c. People now try to understand the customs of those they wish to help.

The Many Voices of India

About sixteen major languages and several hundred dialects are spoken in India. As a result, the Indian government has enormous problems trying to knit together as a nation the many different tribal and religious groups in India.

Delegates attend national conferences and may not always understand what the other delegates say. Different radio networks broadcast the news in fourteen different languages, yet there are many people in India who don't understand any of them.

While India was a part of the British Empire, English was the official language of the government, but only about 2 percent of the Indian people spoke this language. When India gained its independence in 1947, the country's leaders wanted to replace English with an Indian language. They chose Hindi, which is understood by about 50 percent of the people. The Hindi-speaking people live mostly in northern and central India. Most of the people of southern India do not understand Hindi. They resented this choice. In some of India's twenty-seven states, bloody riots were start-ed by groups that wanted to continue using their own languages.

In 1957, the Indian government announced a plan for reorganizing India's twenty-seven states into fourteen new states. These new states corresponded roughly to India's major language areas. Each state could adopt its own major language for official use within the state.

Some groups were still not happy. The state of Bombay had two large groups speaking different languages. So in 1960, the government divided Bombay into two states. The same thing occurred in Punjab in 1966. Since that time, several other groups have also been given their own sates, until India now has 25 states.

In 1967, the government voted to continue using English as an "associate" language along with Hindi for official business. The government backed a plan by which all Indian children would learn three languages: the official language of the state, Hindi, and English. Today, most educated Indians speak English, so until Indians can agree upon a common language, English may serve as a link to bind them together.

1. When India was part of the Empire, the official language was
    a. Hindi.   c. Chinese.
    b. French.   d. English.

2. The word in paragraph 1 that means *separate forms of a language, each belonging to an area or group of people* is _____.

3. The words "as an 'associate' language" in the last paragraph describe the word

    _____.

4. While it is not directly stated, the article suggests that
    a. everyone in India can speak and understand the English language.
    b. language is sometimes a barrier among the people of India.
    c. it is hard for the Indian people to learn Hindi.

5. The Hindi-speaking people live mostly in
    a. northern and central India.
    b. southern India.
    c. rural India.

6. On the whole, the article tells about
    a. reorganizing official business in Hindi.
    b. the confusion of languages in India.
    c. the problem Indians have in knitting.

7. Which statement does this article lead you to believe?
    a. Indians feel all their problems can be solved by the English.
    b. India has many problems that will take a long time to solve.
    c. The Indian government has very few problems left to solve.

8. Why did the people of southern India resent the choice of Hindi?
    a. It sounded too much like English.
    b. Most of them did not understand it.
    c. They preferred to speak in Swahili.

9. Think about the concept for this group of articles. Which statement seems true both for the article and for the concept?
    a. India should progress more quickly when it has a common language.
    b. The Indian government is not interested in using a common language.
    c. Indian children are not expected to learn their own language.

Up by Their Bootstraps

The Spanish name *Puerto Rico* means "rich port." Despite its name, in the mid-twentieth century Puerto Rico was anything but rich. The island was densely populated, especially in the urban areas. Its climate was ideal for farming, but much of the land had been depleted by soil erosion. There was little industry. No useful minerals were mined, and few tourists came to enjoy the beautiful beaches because there were no good hotels.

Then in the early 1940s, far-sighted Puerto Rican and United States leaders devised "Operation Bootstrap" to improve the island's economy. (When people say, "Pull yourself up by your bootstraps," they mean *solve your own problems.*) With technical and financial assistance from the United States, Puerto Rico attacked its problems in several different ways.

Tax benefits and low-rent buildings were offered to investors who would build factories in Puerto Rico. Improved educational opportunities reduced illiteracy and helped prepare Puerto Ricans for jobs.

A land distribution program broke up large estates and created small farms. Farmers learned to plant different kinds of crops and to use contour planting to control soil erosion.

Slums were replaced by houses and apartments. Then a modern resort hotel was built. The island, with its exceptional climate, became a popular vacation place. Investors eagerly built more hotels.

Operation Bootstrap saw political as well as economic gains. In 1947, Puerto Ricans gained the right to elect their own governor. In 1952, Puerto Rico wrote its own constitution and became a self-governing commonwealth of the United States.

Today Puerto Rico is the wealthiest of the Caribbean islands. Its service industries account for most of the island's income, manufacturing is second in importance, and the balance comes from agriculture. However, with 1,000 people per square mile—more than any state in the United States—there is still much overcrowding and poverty. And although industrialization has done much to create jobs, the unemployment rate is three times higher than in the United States.

So while gains have been dramatic, serious problems remain. Perhaps because of this, Puerto Ricans have yet to make a final decision about whether to remain a commonwealth, to apply for U.S. statehood, or to become an independent nation.

1. The name *Puerto Rico* in English means
   a. poor sport.
   b. rich port.
   c. army fort.
   d. red quart.

2. The word in paragraph 2 that means *thought up* is _____.

3. The words "depleted by soil erosion" in paragraph 1 describe
   _____.

4. While it is not directly stated, the article suggests that
   a. investors were encouraged to start many new farms.
   b. all the people of Puerto Rico are still farmers.
   c. there are many skilled workers in Puerto Rico today.

5. A modern resort hotel was built to
   a. attract tourists.
   b. reduce illiteracy.
   c. help the farmers.

6. On the whole, the article tells about
   a. the right place to build a resort hotel.
   b. government officials who wear bootstraps.
   c. attempts to improve Puerto Rico's economy.

7. Which statement does this article lead you to believe?
   a. The income of Puerto Ricans has dropped steadily since the 1940s.
   b. The income level of Puerto Ricans does not matter.
   c. The income level of Puerto Ricans will continue to improve.

8. Why did leaders of Puerto Rico and the United States plan "Operation Bootstrap"?
   a. They wanted to improve the island's economy.
   b. They had an overproduction of bootstraps.
   c. They wanted to reduce the island's efficiency.

9. Think about the concept for this group of articles. Which statement seems true both for the article and for the concept?
   a. Education and planning have improved the lives of many Puerto Ricans.
   b. Education is not important for people who have very low incomes.
   c. Operation Bootstrap was not well planned.

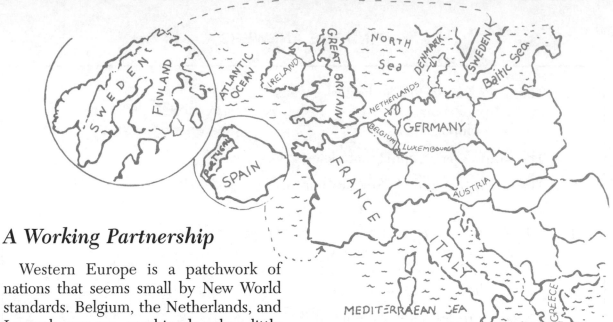

A Working Partnership

Western Europe is a patchwork of nations that seems small by New World standards. Belgium, the Netherlands, and Luxembourg are, combined, only a little larger than West Virginia. France is smaller than Texas. These countries have had a long history of wars over boundaries, jealousies, and competition. But some of these age-old barriers are crumbling, and national leaders are learning to work together.

At the end of World War II, most European industry lay in ruins. European leaders reasoned that economic recovery would be speeded up if manufacturers could buy and sell freely across national boundaries. Therefore, in 1957, Belgium, France, the Netherlands, Luxembourg, Italy, and West Germany formed a cooperative economic union called the Common Market that did away with import duties and other trade barriers among member nations. It allowed certain kinds of workers to move more freely from one member nation to another.

The Common Market was so successful that Ireland, the United Kingdom, and Denmark joined in 1973, followed in 1981 by Greece, and in 1986 by Spain and Portugal. In 1992, the name was changed to the European Union and a new treaty was signed. Austria, Sweden, and Finland joined in 1995, bringing the number of member nations to fifteen.

Following the dissolution of the former Soviet Union, many countries in Eastern Europe began seeking membership in the European Union. Membership is certain to be granted to some of these countries, but requirements for new members are strict. Among other things, countries seeking admission to the European Union must reduce inflation and political corruption, and they must modernize their financial operations.

The treaty that created the European Union also provided for the creation of a common currency and a central European bank for all member nations. While there is acceptance of economic cooperation among the member nations, it is uncertain whether all the member nations will agree to a unified currency.

120

1. Western Europe is a patchwork of
   a. large nations.
   b. jealous nations.
   c. small nations.
   d. warring nations.

2. The word in paragraph 4 that means *rigorous* is _____.

3. The words "age-old barriers" in paragraph 1 refer to the small nations'

   _____.

4. While it is not directly stated, the article suggests that
   a. wars were destroying the economy of small nations.
   b. there are not enough small nations in Europe.
   c. arguments between nations are best settled by trade barriers.

5. The cooperative economic union that began after World War II eventually became the
   a. Soviet Union.
   b. European Union.
   c. United Kingdom.

6. On the whole, the article tells about
   a. developing economic cooperation among European nations.
   b. creating trade barriers to help economic recovery.
   c. ruining the economy of Western Europe.

7. Which statement does this article lead you to believe?
   a. The economy of the European Union is weak.
   b. Members of a cooperative economic union cannot compete for trade.
   c. In order to help themselves, nations are helping each other.

8. Why was a cooperative economic union formed after World War II?
   a. European leaders wanted to speed economic recovery.
   b. European leaders had not thought of it earlier.
   c. The leaders of the six founding nations became friends during the war.

9. Think about the concept for this group of articles. Which statement seems true both for the article and for the concept?
   a. As the European Union grows, its members may plan to cooperate in other matters.
   b. The nations of Europe do not wish to compete with the United States.
   c. The continent of Europe consists of six nations.

Eyes in the Sky

Map makers have to work fast to keep up with rapid changes on the face of Earth. New highways and bridges are built. Dams form new lakes. Almost overnight, new housing and factories fan out around large cities. To be useful, maps must be revised constantly to show these changes.

Map makers have used a handy tool that helps them keep up with the changes. Aerial photography quickly and accurately collects information about the face of Earth.

Map-making planes carry cameras that point straight down. Each photograph shows one small, square part of Earth's surface, but the camera takes many over-lapping photographs as the plane flies back and forth over the area to be mapped. Later, these photos are carefully trimmed and fitted together.

An aerial camera can see some things not visible from ground level. It can look down through water and map submarine canyons and the limits of the continental shelf. It can map rock formations not apparent on the surface. With special film, it can spot where water or oil deposits may lie under the surface.

Aerial photographs from planes are good, but airplanes can fly only so high. When satellite technology became available, a series of satellites was designed to map Earth from space. Landsat 1 was launched in 1972, followed by Landsats 2, 3, 4, 5, 6 (which was lost in space), and in 1978, Landsat 7.

The Landsat series was designed to take pictures of Earth using special devices called a scanner and a thematic mapper. Landsat images are extremely detailed, which makes them useful for farmers, city planners, and environmentalists. And now, maps can be updated in an instant. This satellite technology can describe our changing Earth much better than could the earlier photographs taken by airplanes at lower altitudes.

1. Some aerial cameras are mounted on
    a. satellites.
    b. dams and bridges.
    c. thematic mappers.
    d. the continental shelf.

2. The word in paragraph 3 that means *covering and stretching beyond* is
    _____.

3. The words "extremely detailed" in paragraph 6 describe
    _____.

4. While it is not directly stated, the article suggests that
    a. old maps gave too much information.
    b. old maps are better than new ones.
    c. old maps were not completely accurate.

5. Cameras in space can send photographs to Earth showing
    a. whole continents.
    b. water under Earth's surface.
    c. eyes up in the sky.

6. On the whole, the article tells about
    a. new housing and factories around large cities.
    b. rock formations that show where water may lie.
    c. aerial methods used in map making.

7. Which statement does this article lead you to believe?
    a. The aerial camera is used to make automatic mapping machines.
    b. Aerial views are giving us a clear picture of our planet.
    c. The aerial camera answers all of our questions about Earth.

8. Why are the pictures from the Landsat series better than earlier pictures?
    a. They don't use a scanner.
    b. They map Earth from space.
    c. They include photos of airplanes.

9. Think about the concept for this group of articles. Which statement seems true both for the article and for the concept?
    a. Modern map makers have to travel a lot.
    b. Modern map making is helped by new technology.
    c. Modern map makers use prehistoric maps.

A Harvest for the Future

Unlike many plants, trees grow slowly. Thirty to eighty years are necessary before a tree grows to the right size for harvesting as lumber or pulpwood. But a tree crop can be a good investment for a landowner or farmer, since trees will grow on the parts of his land where ordinary crops will not grow.

Trees do much more than provide lumber for home building. They provide raw materials for making paper, plastics, synthetics, turpentine, and other products. Even more important, trees protect the nation's water supply by holding back erosion and keeping water in the soil.

America once had huge natural forests. To start their farms, pioneers cleared many trees. Later, logging crews employed by lumber companies moved into other forests. They cut all the valuable trees, and then moved on.

There were few efforts to protect our forests or to plant new ones until the beginning of the present century. Then, together with forest experts, government officials, and landowners, the lumber companies began planning to support the planting of new forests. The American Tree Farm System, begun during World War II, is one of the plans that grew out of this cooperation.

Landowners who wish to establish tree farms can get help from a professional, state-employed forester, or from an association of lumber companies. They can get advice on what kind of trees to plant and how to care for them. Landowners must protect their trees by keeping grazing animals away and by removing dead or diseased trees. They must keep replanting, so that young trees are growing at all times to replace those ready for cutting.

Some tree farms are small woodlots. Others cover thousands of acres. All together, they are of great value to the United States and its people.

1. For a tree to grow large enough for harvesting may take
    a. eleven to fifteen months.
    c. ten to twenty days.
    b. five to six years.
    d. thirty to eighty years.

2. The word in paragraph 2 that means *the wearing away of the earth* is

    _____ .

3. The words "unlike many plants" in paragraph 1 refer to _____ .

4. While it is not directly stated, the article suggests that
    a. trees can be destroyed in many ways.
    b. trees were preserved by our pioneers.
    c. huge forests can be found everywhere.

5. A landowner who wants to start a tree farm can get help from a
    a. harvester.
    b. foreigner.
    c. forester.

6. On the whole, the article tells about
    a. making finished products from raw materials.
    b. planting and protecting our valuable trees.
    c. an association formed by lumber companies.

7. Which statement does this article lead you to believe?
    a. The American Tree Farm System was begun by early pioneers.
    b. Landowners must belong to an association of lumber companies.
    c. Many different people are concerned with saving the land.

8. Why did pioneers clear the trees from some forests?
    a. They needed clear land to start their farms.
    b. They didn't like the way the trees were growing.
    c. The pioneers needed the exercise to stay strong.

9. Think about the concept for this group of articles. Which statement seems true both for the article and for the concept?
    a. Grazing animals cannot do any harm to young growing plants.
    b. People have always understood the danger of clearing too much land.
    c. People today have a better understanding of their environment.

More Than Flood Control

The Tennessee River Basin is an area of 40,000 square miles that includes parts of seven states, from Kentucky to Alabama. In the early 1930s, the Tennessee basin was a land of floods, eroded farms, and cut-over forests. There were few industries, unemployment was widespread, and most people in the area were very poor.

In 1933 something happened to change all that. A government agency — the Tennessee Valley Authority — was formed to put the river to work helping the people.

The heart of the TVA plan was the building of thirty dams on the Tennessee River and its tributaries. The dams served many different purposes. They provided a deeper channel, so that freight barges and other boats could use the river. They generated low-priced electric power. They prevented floods and they formed new lakes that could be used for boating and fishing.

The TVA plan went beyond merely putting the river to work. Farmers were taught better ways of plowing to control erosion. They were provided with low-cost fertilizers. Seedling trees were planted to replace the cut-over forests.

Within a few years, the whole area benefited. New factories were built to take advantage of the water transportation and electric power. The factories provided jobs. They paid taxes that were used in turn to build better schools and better roads. New parks and boat docks brought visitors to the lakes, providing still more new sources of income. Today, those seedling trees have grown into valuable forests.

The TVA plan was a long-range plan that went far beyond solving the problem of flood control. It improved the land and restored much of its beauty. It raised the economy of an entire area.

1. The Tennessee River Basin includes parts of seven states from
      a. Canarsie to Arizona.   c. Canada to Alaska.
      b. Kentucky to Alabama.   d. Kansas to Alabama.

2. The word in paragraph 3 that means *streams that flow into a main river system*

   is _____ .

3. The words "an entire area" in paragraph 6 tell about an _____ .

4. While it is not directly stated, the article suggests that
      a. sometimes people can make nature work for them.
      b. the natural environment can never be changed.
      c. it is wrong to put a river to work for people.

5. The whole area benefited
      a. in less than a month.
      b. within a few years.
      c. after twelve days.

6. On the whole, the article tells about
      a. the benefits that resulted from the Tennessee Valley Authority.
      b. the poor planning that was caused by a Tennessee River Authority.
      c. different government agencies and the tasks they perform.

7. Which statement does this article lead you to believe?
      a. Many different studies were necessary for the TVA plan.
      b. It is not up to people to beautify the land they use.
      c. It is not important for land to be improved at this time.

8. Why were farmers able to control erosion?
      a. The rains stopped for several years.
      b. They had low-priced electric power.
      c. They learned better ways of plowing.

9. Think about the concept for this group of articles. Which statement seems true both for the article and for the concept?
      a. Good planning has many wide-range benefits.
      b. It is better for things to happen naturally.
      c. Too many changes are not good for people.

The River That Won't Be Conquered

The great Mississippi River has served well the people who live near it. But it has also been their enemy. From time to time, heavy rains or melting snows have caused the river to swell and overflow its banks. In the past, such floods have taken many lives. They have destroyed millions of dollars in crops and property.

Planning ways to control floods is the task of the United States Corps of Engineers. In the 1800s, the engineers tried to wall in the river downstream by building a levee that was larger than the Great Wall of China. But after a disastrous flood in 1927, people came to realize that much more flood control was needed. Using giant barges and huge suction dredges that could scoop the earth from the river bed, the Corps of Engineers then set to work on enormous flood control projects.

The engineers built new levees. The levees were from 30 to 50 feet high. They extended up the Mississippi and its tributaries for more than 3,000 miles. In some places, the Mississippi was shallow and flooded easily. The engineers dredged out these shallow places until they were at least 12 feet deep. They also built canals which could carry floodwaters away from the river and into the Gulf of Mexico. Dams were built on the Mississippi's tributaries to hold back excess water.

Left to nature, rivers will endlessly shift their banks. Because of the size and importance of the Mississippi River, engineers decided that its channel should be permanently fixed. To do this, they constructed levees of earth reinforced with metal cable from Cairo in southern Illinois, to Baton Rouge, Louisiana. Yet all their planning was washed away in the record floods of 1993 when Mother Nature and Old Man River teamed up to show who is really in charge!

128

1. In the 1800s, engineers built a levee larger than the
   a. tributaries.
   c. 3,000 miles.
   b. length of the river.
   d. Great Wall of China.

2. The word in paragraph 2 that means *bringing great misfortune* is
   _____.

3. The words "earth reinforced with metal cable " in paragraph 4 describe
   _____.

4. While it is not directly stated, the article suggests that
   a. flood control is a simple thing to accomplish.
   b. engineers can only control smaller rivers.
   c. engineers will have to come up with better plans for controlling the Mississippi.

5. In some places, the Mississippi was
   a. shallow.
   b. shrunken.
   c. silent.

6. On the whole, the article tells about
   a. reinforcing levees with metal cables.
   b. building canals on the Gulf of Mexico.
   c. attempting to control floods along the Mississippi.

7. Which statement does this article lead you to believe?
   a. A large river is a very powerful and complex system.
   b. The Mississippi never caused any severe damage.
   c. The Corps of Engineers needs better training.

8. Why were dams built on the Mississippi's tributaries?
   a. They helped to fill the Mississippi with water.
   b. The dams were built to hold back excess water.
   c. Dams look better when built on the tributaries.

9. Think about the concept for this group of articles. Which statement seems true both for the article and for the concept?
   a. Technical knowledge will not help today's engineers at all.
   b. Reliable flood control is still in the future.
   c. The builders of the Great Wall of China knew more than today's engineers.

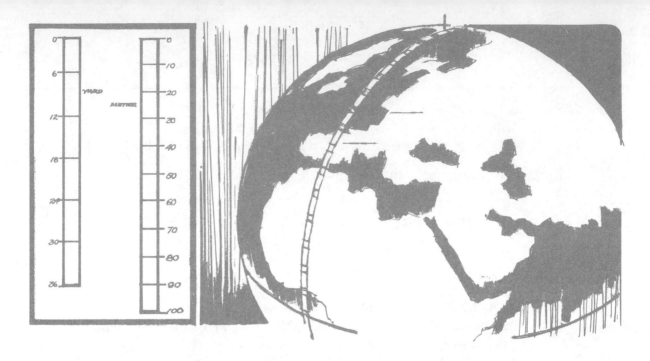

How Long Is a Meter?

The search for standards of accurate measurement has been going on for a long time. Today, accurate measurement is more important than ever before. The size of parts for precision machines and scientific instruments must be controlled carefully. A mistake of one-millionth of an inch in the parts of a spacecraft gyroscope is costly. It could cause a spacecraft aimed at the moon to miss by 1,000 miles.

Ideal standards of measurement are based on things in the natural world that do not change. Such standards can be copied accurately in different parts of the world, at different times.

French scientists were thinking along this line when, in 1799, they decided on the meter as a new unit of length. A meter was one ten-millionth of the distance between the north pole and the equator. The first standard meter was measured along a line fixed between Dunkirk, France and Barcelona, Spain.

The new meter proved a handy unit for measuring length. But making metal bars an exact meter long by computing one-fourth of Earth's circumference and then dividing by 10 million proved awkward. It was easier to make accurate meter bars by comparing them with a master unit. The master unit was a meter bar made of a platinum-iridium alloy. From 1889 until 1960, this bar served as the standard for all other meter bars.

In 1960, the General Conference of Weights and Measures met in Paris and decided on a new standard meter better suited to modern needs. But this meter proved difficult to replicate. Therefore, in 1983, scientists devised a new standard based on the speed of light. A meter is now defined as the distance that light travels in a vacuum in 1/299792458 of a second. The advantage of this new measurement is that it can be reproduced in any well-equipped laboratory in the world.

1. The first standard meter was measured along a line fixed between
   a. Dunkirk and Barcelona.
   b. Paris and Dunkirk.
   c. Barcelona and Spain.
   d. the north pole and the equator.

2. The word in paragraph 4 that means *figuring by arithmetic* is

   _____.

3. The words "better suited to modern needs" in paragraph 5 describe

   _____.

4. While it is not directly stated, the article suggests that
   a. measurements cannot be based on things in the natural world.
   b. French scientists decided the old standards were the best.
   c. modern needs require that measurements be very accurate.

5. It was easier to make accurate meter bars by
   a. copying standards around the world.
   b. daily measurements of the equator.
   c. comparing them with a master unit.

6. On the whole, the article tells about
   a. dividing Earth's circumference.
   b. establishing a standard measure of length.
   c. the General Conference of Weights and Measures.

7. Which statement does this article lead you to believe?
   a. Only one-fourth of Earth's circumference can be measured.
   b. Mistakes in calculation can have serious effects on many things.
   c. Standard meters are impossible to measure in modern times.

8. Why is a mistake of one-millionth of an inch in a gyroscope costly?
   a. It can cause an astronaut to lose a spacecraft.
   b. It can make a spacecraft miss its mark by 1,000 miles.
   c. Industry pays for making precision machines by the inch.

9. Think about the concept for this group of articles. Which statement seems true both for the article and for the concept?
   a. The Conference could not decide upon a new standard.
   b. It is very difficult to measure the speed of light.
   c. Scientists planned the new standard measurement.

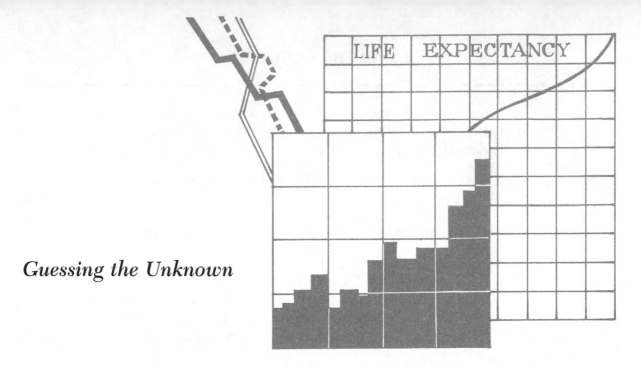

Guessing the Unknown

Suppose you had nothing better to do than flip a coin one million times. If you kept careful records of the million flips, your records would be called statistics. From your statistics, you might say, "A coin flipped a million times will come up heads about half the time." Your statement would be based on the Theory of Probability.

The Theory of Probability predicts only general truths. It does not predict single facts. For example, just because a coin lands heads up once does not mean that it will land tails up the next time. But the greater the number of times the coin is flipped, the greater the probability that half of the time the coin will land heads up.

Science and business often depend on the Theory of Probability. For instance, life insurance companies would like to know how long each insured person is likely to live. The Theory of Probability allows some general predictions. From life-span statistics, an insurance company can predict about how many people in different countries will die each year at a certain age.

To draw up life-span statistics and set fair rates, insurance companies employ mathematicians called actuaries. An actuary must revise the statistics constantly because life-spans are affected by many different things. In 1900, for example, the average life-span in the United States was estimated to be 46.3 years for men and 48.3 years for women. Improved medical care has steadily increased the average life-span. For the year 2000, the averages are estimated at 73.5 years for men and 80.4 years for women.

The person who buys life insurance is planning ahead. Actuaries must depend on accurate statistics and the Theory of Probability to plan even further ahead. In that way, life insurance companies can set fair rates for the buyers and make a fair profit from the insurance they sell.

FIND THE ANSWERS

1. Insurance companies employ mathematicians called
   - a. actuaries.
   - b. activists.
   - c. astrologists.
   - d. aviaries.

2. The word in paragraph 2 that means *foretell* is _____.

3. The words "To draw up life-span statistics and set fair rates" in paragraph 4 refer to the _____.

4. While it is not directly stated, the article suggests that
   - a. a person's life-span may depend on the age in which he or she lives.
   - b. insurance companies can accurately predict anyone's future.
   - c. your life-span depends on how many times you can flip a coin.

5. In 1900, the estimated average life-span for a woman in the United States was
   - a. 99.0 years.
   - b. 73.5 years.
   - c. 48.3 years.

6. On the whole, the article tells about
   - a. using the Theory of Probability in a business.
   - b. actuaries who revise their statistics now and then.
   - c. improved medical care in the United States in 1900.

7. Which statement does this article lead you to believe?
   - a. More people reach old age in today's world.
   - b. The Theory of Probability keeps people alive.
   - c. Insurance companies are against medical care.

8. Why has the life-span estimate increased during the past century?
   - a. It increased the insurance companies' profits.
   - b. Actuaries made better guesses about life-spans.
   - c. Improved medical care increased the estimate.

9. Think about the concept for this group of articles. Which statement seems true both for the article and for the concept?
   - a. The Theory of Probability predicts only single facts.
   - b. The insurance business is built on planned predictions.
   - c. Statistics cannot be based on the life-span of people.

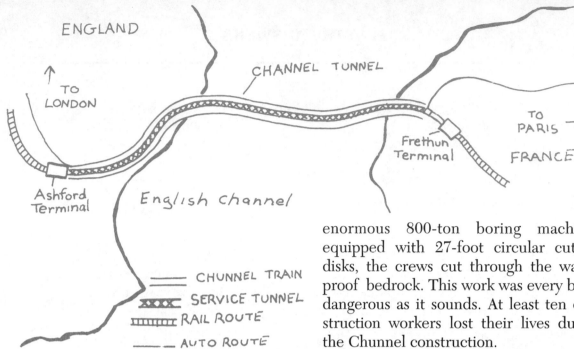

ENGLAND

CHANNEL TUNNEL

↑ TO LONDON

TO PARIS →

Frethun Terminal

FRANCE

Ashford Terminal

English Channel

———— CHUNNEL TRAIN
XXXX SERVICE TUNNEL
ⅢⅢⅢ RAIL ROUTE
——— — AUTO ROUTE

Chunnelling Through

For years, the only way to get from Paris to London was by water or by air. Now, thanks to one of the largest civil engineering projects of the twentieth century, it is possible to make this trip by train through a tunnel under the English Channel.

Construction on the Channel Tunnel, or Chunnel as it is often referred to, began in December 1987. The project took seven years and cost $16 billion—more than double the original estimated price.

The Chunnel is actually three tunnels: two train tunnels set 100 feet apart with a service tunnel between them. Construction crews worked from both sides of the Channel to dig these tunnels 146 feet beneath the chalk bedrock, which lies under the English Channel. Using enormous 800-ton boring machines equipped with 27-foot circular cutting disks, the crews cut through the water-proof bedrock. This work was every bit as dangerous as it sounds. At least ten construction workers lost their lives during the Chunnel construction.

The Chunnel, which opened in November 1994, runs for 31 miles between Ashford, England, and Fréthun, France; 23.6 of those miles are under the English Channel. This makes it the longest undersea tunnel ever built.

The entire trip from London to Paris takes only three hours, which is faster than flying if you count the time to and from airports.

The tunnel portion of the trip takes about 30 minutes. Even at top speed, the ride is smooth.

In addition to the London-Paris train, there is a half-mile-long shuttle train, known as "Le Shuttle," which ferries cars, trucks, and motorcycles between Folke-stone and Calais.

Each passenger train can carry 800 passengers. Each shuttle train can carry 180 cars. In the early years of the twenty-first century, trains are scheduled to depart every 12 minutes and are expected to carry 44 million passengers a year.

1. In 1994, the Chunnel began offering passenger train service
   a. between London and Madrid.
   c. under the English Channel.
   b. between Paris and Rome.
   d. under the Baltic Sea.

2. The word in paragraph 3 that means *solid foundation rock* is
   _____.

3. The words "equipped with 27-foot circular cutting disks" in paragraph 3 refer to _____.

4. While it is not directly stated, the article suggests that
   a. economic relations between England and the Continent will improve.
   b. you can drive your car through the Chunnel.
   c. eventually airlines will go out of business.

5. The tunnel boring machines
   a. broke down frequently.
   b. had 27-foot cutting disks.
   c. could not cut through chalk.

6. On the whole, the article tells about
   a. the dangers of underwater tunnel construction.
   b. a new way to travel between London and Paris.
   c. trains that travel faster than the speed of sound.

7. Which statement does this article lead you to believe?
   a. The best way to cross a body of water is by ferry.
   b. The Chunnel is in danger of collapsing.
   c. The Chunnel will end England's separation from the rest of Europe.

8. Why is the Chunnel train faster than flying?
   a. There is no wind resistance under water.
   b. The lines are shorter.
   c. Passengers avoid traveling to and from airports.

9. Think about the concept for this group of articles. Which statement seems true both for the article and for the concept?
   a. In the age of jet engines, train travel is no longer practical.
   b. People will continue to need safe, efficient means of travel.
   c. The English are the only people who will benefit from the Chunnel.

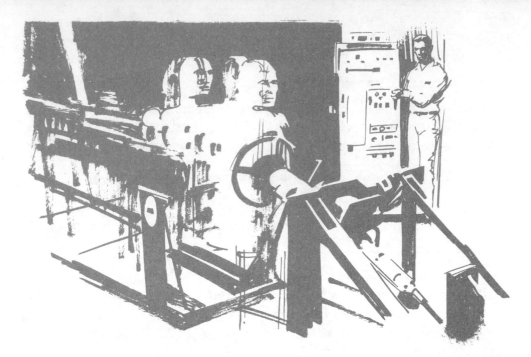

Planning for Safety

The number of cars, trucks, and buses on American highways is rapidly increasing. As roads become more crowded, auto accidents are increasing, too. By 1997, traffic accidents were causing more than 42,000 deaths a year. Millions more motorists were being injured.

As the toll climbed, many groups worked to make highway travel safer. Highway planners designed safer roads, while educators tried to make drivers more safety-minded. Automotive engineers concentrated on making cars safer.

The engineers made a study of auto accidents. They learned that in many crashes, the passengers' bodies are thrown forward. The driver is likely to be thrown onto the steering column, which may go through the chest. Other passengers may strike the windshield, receiving head injuries or serious cuts if the glass breaks. When a car is struck from the rear, passengers' heads are snapped backward often causing neck injuries.

As a result of this kind of study, all new cars, beginning in 1964, were equipped with seat belts. Many states have passed laws requiring drivers and passengers to wear seat belts, but it is estimated that only 68 percent of Americans do so. Some people are now urging all 50 states to pass laws that will require everyone in a car to wear a seat belt and that will prohibit children under the age of 13 from riding in the front seat of a car.

In 1986, another safety feature—the air bag—was introduced. Air bags were designed to inflate at speeds of up to 200 miles per hour during a crash, thus protecting the occupants of the car. Ironically, this safety device proved to be fatal to some people—most of them children—for whom the air bags were too powerful. The National Highway Traffic Safety Administration believes that as many as 65 percent of air-bag related deaths of children could be prevented by using less powerful air bags. However, it recommends continued use of the more powerful air bags for adults.

Tens of thousands of lives and billions of dollars can be saved every year by careful planning and the use of safety devices.

1. Since 1964 all new cars have been equipped with
   a. headrests.
   b. windshields.
   c. stronger sides.
   d. seat belts.

2. The word in paragraph 5 that means *contrary to expectations* is
   _____.

3. The words "designed to inflate at speeds of up to 200 miles per hour" in paragraph 5 refer to _____.

4. While it is not directly stated, the article suggests that
   a. some accidents can be avoided.
   b. accidents are good for business.
   c. accidents are required by Congress.

5. The number of cars on our highways will continue to
   a. be baglike.
   b. increase.
   c. decrease.

6. On the whole, the article tells about
   a. traffic accidents in the year 1986.
   b. different kinds of drivers.
   c. automotive safety devices.

7. Which statement does this article lead you to believe?
   a. The more crowded the roads are, the fewer accidents happen.
   b. Nobody cares when people are hurt or killed in accidents.
   c. Many different groups are concerned about traffic injuries.

8. Why are seat belts important when properly fastened?
   a. They prevent car doors from flying open during an accident.
   b. They prevent many injuries and reduce the severity of others.
   c. They keep passengers from leaving the scene of an accident.

9. Think about the concept for this group of articles. Which statement seems true both for the article and for the concept?
   a. The increase in travel makes better safety measures a necessity.
   b. In America accidents only happen on highways where tolls are paid.
   c. New cars should not be required to install any safety devices.

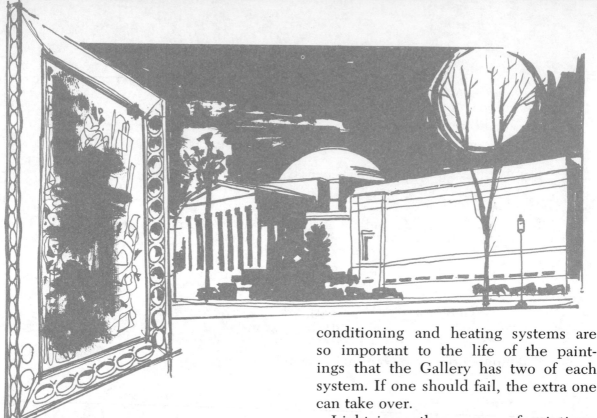

Nature Is Their Enemy

The National Gallery of Art in Washington, D.C., is one of the world's greatest art museums. Millions of persons have entered its doors to see paintings by the world's fine artists. But if these priceless masterpieces are to be preserved, the Gallery must protect them carefully. The Gallery's 135 guards have successfully prevented damage and theft, but protecting the paintings from nature is a greater problem.

In past times, the owners of paintings did not protect them from damaging changes in humidity and temperature. As a result, the life-spans of these paintings were shortened. In the National Gallery, however, humidity and temperature are carefully controlled. The building is air-conditioned in summer and heated in winter. The air-conditioning and heating systems are so important to the life of the paintings that the Gallery has two of each system. If one should fail, the extra one can take over.

Light is another enemy of paintings. Ultraviolet rays in light cause paintings to fade. Long ago, paintings often hung in dark churches and palaces. A coat of varnish was a protection from the weak light. But when museums took over the care of many paintings, they were often hung in brighter light than before. Soon they were in danger of fading. The damaging effects of light were increased when the museums removed the varnish coating, yellowed with age.

To protect its paintings, the National Gallery installed a special kind of glass in its skylights. This glass allows visible light to enter the building but it keeps out harmful ultraviolet rays. The Gallery has also developed new and better varnishes which help to keep paintings from fading. Thanks to these new precautions, many of the world's greatest paintings are being preserved for future generations to enjoy.

FIND THE ANSWERS

1. Ultraviolet rays in light cause paintings to
   a. fade. c. glare.
   b. glow. d. fall.

2. The word in the last paragraph that means *care taken ahead of time* is

   _____.

3. The words "in dark churches and palaces" in paragraph 3 tell about the

   _____.

4. While it is not directly stated, the article suggests that
   a. great artists painted with coats of new varnish.
   b. humidity and temperature cannot affect paintings.
   c. some priceless paintings were not preserved.

5. The National Gallery of Art is in
   a. Wappington, L.I.
   b. Wilmington, N.C.
   c. Washington, D.C.

6. On the whole, the article tells about
   a. preserving millions of persons in buildings.
   b. protecting great paintings from nature.
   c. painting dark churches and palaces.

7. Which statement does this article lead you to believe?
   a. Too much fuss is made about paintings that were done long ago.
   b. The care of the world's greatest paintings is a big responsibility.
   c. The National Gallery is the only museum that contains paintings.

8. Why did the museums remove varnish coatings from some paintings?
   a. The coatings had yellowed with age.
   b. They wanted the paintings to fade.
   c. The coatings were beginning to peel.

9. Think about the concept for this group of articles. Which statement seems true both for the article and for the concept?
   a. The National Gallery's 135 guards protect thieves.
   b. Ultraviolet rays are permitted to enter the National Gallery.
   c. Modern art galleries must plan their buildings carefully.

Putting the Arts Together

Three important things happened in 1955 in New York City. The Metropolitan Opera Association looked for a place to build a new opera house, since its old building was inadequate. The New York Philharmonic Orchestra was told that its old building would soon be torn down. Like the opera, the orchestra needed a new home. The city announced plans to clear a three-block slum area, as part of an urban renewal project.

To some people, the three things seemed to fit together. Why not build new homes, they asked, for both opera and orchestra, on the cleared slum site? Why not develop the area as a unified grouping of theaters and concert halls?

A committee of public-spirited citizens started work on plans for such a project. They named it the Lincoln Center for the Performing Arts. Architects drew up an overall plan for the site.

Five large buildings were planned for Lincoln Center: Avery Fisher Hall, for the philharmonic orchestra; the new Metropolitan Opera House; the New York State Theater, for ballet and light opera; the Vivian Beaumont Theater, for plays; and the Juilliard School where musicians, actors, and dancers would study. There would also be a library-museum, a bandshell for outdoor concerts, a fountain, and a reflecting pool.

Six different architectural firms were hired to design the buildings. They met together once a month, to make sure that each building would be in harmony with the overall plan.

Early in 1959, President Eisenhower broke ground for the first of the buildings. Ten years later, workers were completing the last of them. The dingy, rat-infested tenements were gone. In their places stood gleaming theaters and tree-shaded plazas. Today, all New York uses and enjoys its new and exciting Lincoln Center for education and entertainment.

FIND THE ANSWERS

1. The Lincoln Center is in
   a. New Haven.
   b. New York.
   c. the Metropolitan.
   d. New Mexico.

2. The word in paragraph 1 that means *having to do with the city* is

   _____.

3. The words "of public-spirited citizens" in paragraph 3 describe a

   _____.

4. While it is not directly stated, the article suggests that
   a. there are many slums in a big city.
   b. cities have very few slum areas.
   c. slum areas can never be cleared up.

5. The Juilliard School is for
   a. educators.
   b. musicians.
   c. opera.

6. On the whole, the article tells about
   a. the New York Philharmonic Orchestra.
   b. ground-breaking by President Eisenhower.
   c. an entertainment area that replaced a slum.

7. Which statement does this article lead you to believe?
   a. Entertainment at the Lincoln Center is quite varied.
   b. All you can see at the Lincoln Center is the ballet.
   c. A school does not belong at an entertainment center.

8. Why did six architectural firms meet once a month?
   a. They liked looking at themselves in the reflecting pool.
   b. They could not agree on the architecture of the buildings.
   c. They wanted to be sure all the buildings were in harmony.

9. Think about the concept for this group of articles. Which statement seems true both for the article and for the concept?
   a. Theaters and tree-shaded plazas cannot replace all tenements.
   b. A city can be made beautiful with the right planning.
   c. The people of New York City did not want the new center.

The
Sword of Light

There once dwelt in Ireland a young lad named Patrick, who dearly loved to bet. He would bet how long it might take a cloud to pass overhead, or what color a stranger's eyes might be. In short, he would bet on anything.

One day Patrick was strolling on a path that meandered through a forest. As he walked, Patrick chanced to spy an old man in a dark glen, playing a solitary game of backgammon. Naturally, Patrick stopped to watch. After a while, he said courteously, "It's begging your pardon I am, sir, but are you betting your left hand against your right hand?"

"That's the way of it," the old man replied. "And it grieves me to think my right hand always wins, for I can only bet on my left hand." He glanced slyly up at Patrick. "Would you care to be making a small wager on one of my hands?"

"Since you're so obliging," Patrick answered, "I'll bet my last sixpence on the right hand."

"Done," the old man said, "and if you win I'll pay you a hundred guineas." He cleared his board and began a new game. In the twinkling of an eye, Patrick was richer by one hundred guineas.

"I'm thinking," Patrick mused to himself as he collected his winnings, "that the old man must be a sorcerer. But sure and that's no affair of mine." And off Patrick went to buy some acreage which he could farm. He worked hard at his farming, but in the back of his mind was the memory of the old man in the dark glen. Well, before you could spell *shillelagh*, Patrick was back in the glen betting again and winning. This time, instead of guineas, Patrick asked for the most beautiful girl in all of Ireland as his bride.

Next morning came a knocking at the farmhouse door, and when Patrick peered out, who should be standing there but the most beautiful girl in the world. "Who are you and how did you get here?" exclaimed Patrick.

"I was sent here by the old man in the glen," said the girl, smiling. "Am I not welcome then?"

"You are more than welcome," Patrick cried. The girl was happy to hear these words and consented to stay.

Sabina was the colleen's name. She and Patrick were married and lived well and happily together until Patrick again bethought himself of the old man in the glen.

"One last game," Patrick reflected, "to win garments of brocade for Sabina, some trinkets for her hair, and maybe an elegant shay to take her into town." That night, when Sabina was fast asleep, Patrick stole away to the glen.

"Have you come to bet on my right hand again?" the old man asked craftily.

"I have," said Patrick, "for Sabina needs garments of brocade, trinkets for her hair, and a shay to take her in style to town."

"She shall have them," said the old man, "if you win. However, should I win the game, I shall want you to fetch me the Sword of Light."

"Gladly," Patrick replied in his well-mannered way, "if you will tell me what it is and where to find it."

"It is far across the sea in a cavern well guarded by a fierce and vicious dragon," the old man answered. "It is sheathed in a dark scabbard and hidden deep inside the cavern. You shall fetch the sword for me, lad, or die trying."

"Only if I lose the game," Patrick reminded him. The old man grinned knowingly, for he had waited long and patiently for this moment.

"I seem to have lost," Patrick said later with great surprise when the game was over. "But surely you did not mean all that palaver about a Sword of Light."

"Mean it I did," the old man said grimly, "and fetch it for me you shall.

And until the Sword of Light is in my possession, you shall not close your eyes again, though you may perish for lack of sleep. One word of caution," the old man added as Patrick stumbled out of the glen. "Do not remove the Sword of Light from its sheath. You must hand the sword to me in its scabbard."

Poor Patrick went home and tried to sleep, but it was as the old man had predicted. Try as he would, Patrick could not close his weary eyes. At last he woke Sabina and told her his sorry tale.

"I am the old man's niece," Sabina said then, "and I can do a little magic of my own. I will help you on one condition, but you must promise me faithfully that you will never bet on anything again." As soon as Patrick promised, Sabina gave him an enchanted horse and a magic harp. She placed her hands lightly over Patrick's ears, saying, "The harp shall play of its own accord, but you shall not hear its melody."

Patrick mounted the magic steed at once and flew off over land and sea to the cavern guarded by the monstrous dragon. As soon as Patrick reached the cave, the harp filled the air with music. Its melody was so haunting and strange that the birds fell silent, and the summer breezes stopped blowing. The dragon wept bitter tears and let Patrick pass without so much as a sideward glance. Quickly Patrick located the Sword of Light, seized it in its scabbard, and remounted his horse. Back he flew to the glen, where the old man was still playing his game of backgammon.

"Now perhaps I can sleep again," the weary Patrick cried, and he began to pull the Sword of Light from its sheath.

"Do not unsheath it, wretched lad!"

the old man shouted in fury. But it was too late, for Patrick had already freed the sword from its scabbard. A blinding light spread throughout the glen. "You have destroyed me," the old man wailed, and he disappeared in a flurry of smoke.

As for Patrick, he rushed home where he fell into a deep sleep that lasted for two days and two nights. When he finally awoke, the new Patrick never bet on anything again.

The Sword of Light, some say, is still there, deep in the woods, filling the glen with a wondrous light, as if the morning sun rises from that very spot. And should you by chance stumble into the light someday, you will see and hear magic no other mortal has ever known.

1087 words

IV

Where Might Change Take Us?

In this section, you will read some of the predictions about how life tomorrow may be lived. You will read about these things in the areas of history, space, biology, anthropology, economics, geography, Earth science, space, mathematics, engineering, and art.

Keep these questions in mind when you are reading.

1. What are some recent changes that may affect all our lives?

2. What things may happen because of recent changes?

3. How will we change as individuals because of things that may happen?

4. What kinds of change would you like to see now?

5. What part could you play in making changes?

Look on pages 11-12 for help with words you don't understand in this section.

One Man's Peaceful War

In the 1950s the Italian architect Danilo Dolci visited western Sicily. It was, he said, "the most wretched piece of country I had ever seen." A long history of ignorance and poverty overshadowed the area, which is part of an island off the Italian coast.

In some villages, the people burned manure rather than spread it on their fields to enrich the soil. They did not understand erosion. They thought that magic spells caused the soil to disappear from their hillside farms. Few people could read and write. Few children went to school. There was almost no industry. Not able to make a living, many people had turned to crime. Some of the politicians who governed the area were themselves criminals who benefited by keeping the people poor and ignorant.

Danilo Dolci gave up a promising career and began to devote his life to helping the Sicilians. He taught them to plan peaceful demonstrations that would call the Italian government's attention to their problems.

Under Dolci's direction, some Sicilians staged a "strike in reverse" by repairing roads—without pay. Dolci advised the people to ask the government for jobs rather than money, for irrigation dams, and for agricultural experts to teach them better ways to farm.

Finally, some constructive help came from the Italian government, and living conditions slowly improved. Over the years since Dolci first arrived, Sicily has been modernized. However, the island's economic development remains dependent on outside assistance and has been further hindered by political instability.

Today, Sicilians are faced with extremely high taxes, recession, and unemployment that is twice as high as the rest of Italy. Many Sicilians are beginning to relearn the lessons of Danilo Dolci. They must take control of their own future—whenever possible without outside assistance.

1. In some villages in western Sicily, the people did not understand
    - a. erosion.
    - c. animals.
    - b. poverty.
    - d. industry.

2. The word in paragraph 1 that means *state of knowing little or nothing* is
    _____.

3. The words "who governed the area were themselves criminals" in paragraph 2
    describe some of the _____.

4. While it is not directly stated, the article suggests that
    - a. ignorant people make the best farmers.
    - b. magicians make trouble for farmers.
    - c. people need to know more about the land.

5. Danilo Dolci gave up a promising career as
    - a. an engineer.
    - b. an architect.
    - c. a politician.

6. On the whole, the article tells about
    - a. one individual's fight to help a group of people.
    - b. large secret groups of troublemakers.
    - c. villagers who work on farms without pay.

7. Which statement does this article lead you to believe?
    - a. One person can never hope to bring about any changes.
    - b. Good planning can help a country progress and grow.
    - c. Ignorance, poverty, and crime make a country strong.

8. What happened as a result of Dolci's actions?
    - a. Living conditions in Sicily improved.
    - b. Many strikes in Sicily were held backward.
    - c. Some magicians in Sicily became agricultural experts.

9. Think about the concept for this group of articles. Which statement seems true
    both for the article and for the concept?
    - a. Individuals may make important contributions to their country.
    - b. Individuals should not try to understand their country's problems.
    - c. Few individuals can really contribute to their country.

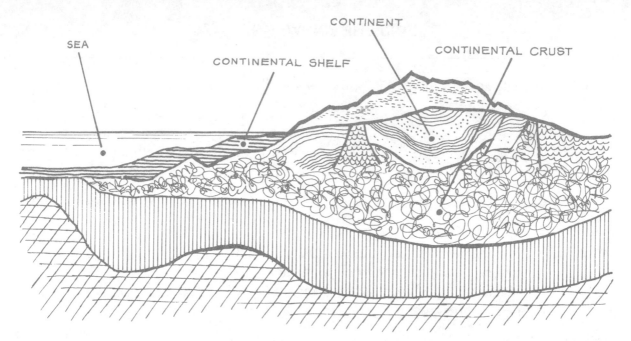

SEA CONTINENTAL SHELF CONTINENT CONTINENTAL CRUST

The Underwater Frontier

Throughout history, many nations have gained land by fighting wars or by sending explorers to plant their flag in newly discovered lands. The strongest nations or those with the most daring explorers usually took possession of new frontiers with all their valuable resources.

One of Earth's remaining frontiers is the ocean floor. Oil and natural gas are already being pumped from undersea wells. Undersea springs may one day provide new supplies of fresh water. Fish, plants, and valuable minerals may be harvested from undersea farms. But who owns the ocean floor?

In 1958, eighty-six nations agreed to a treaty which stated that nations own underwater territory off their coasts to a depth of 656 feet, "or to the depth they are technically able to explore." This means that only coastal nations own the rich continental shelves. It also means that only the most technologically advanced nations can explore the deeper parts of the ocean.

Understandably, landlocked nations began asking that some of the undersea frontier be saved for them. Under the treaty, there would be nothing left for the landlocked nations but the deepest, poorest parts of the sea.

Some people agreed that there should be a fairer distribution of undersea minerals. So the United Nations sponsored a series of meetings from 1973 to 1982. These meetings resulted in another treaty. This treaty calls for member nations to guard against polluting the ocean; for the limits of a nation's undersea territory to be set at 12 nautical miles from its coastline; and for shared development of mineral deposits under the sea, which are to be considered "the common heritage of mankind."

Several signers of the 1958 treaty, including the United States, Japan, Italy, the United Kingdom, and Germany, have refused to ratify the second treaty. Until these differences are worked out, the first treaty is still in force. A uniform Law of the Sea and the solution to the boundary disputes in this watery frontier lie in the future.

148

1. Undersea wells are being pumped for oil and
   a. salt.
   b. minerals.
   c. food plants.
   d. natural gas.

2. The word in paragraph 5 that means *something that can be inherited* is
   _____.

3. The words "off their coasts to a depth of 656 feet" in paragraph 3 refer to
   _____.

4. While it is not directly stated, the article suggests that
   a. most nations have sea coasts of their own.
   b. the ocean floor is one of our last frontiers.
   c. nothing valuable can be found on the ocean floor.

5. Throughout history, nations often gained land by
   a. exploring the ocean floor.
   b. fighting wars.
   c. mining the sea.

6. On the whole, the article tells about
   a. rich and easy-to-explore continental shelves.
   b. valuable undersea land and who shall own it.
   c. daring explorers who own the ocean floor.

7. Which statement does this article lead you to believe?
   a. In earlier days, nations might have gone to war over undersea land.
   b. All valuable resources on land have been used up.
   c. Nations today no longer want to own their own resources.

8. Why are landlocked nations claiming that other nations are unfair?
   a. The other nations won't let the landlocked nations move to the sea.
   b. The landlocked nations are being forced to sell their underwater equipment.
   c. Other nations have left them only the deepest, poorest parts of the sea.

9. Think about the concept for this group of articles. Which statement seems true both for the article and for the concept?
   a. The only food that anyone can expect to get from the sea is fish.
   b. Someday, undersea land may produce great benefits for all people.
   c. Food from undersea farms will taste salty.

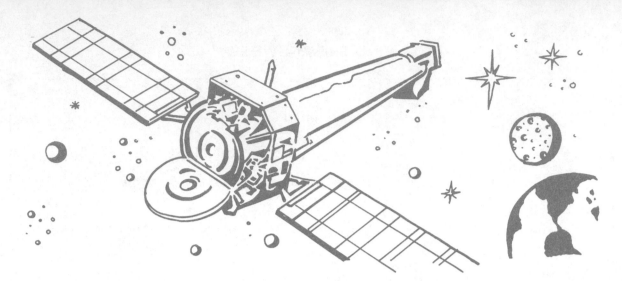

Looking Outward

A scientist once said that studying the stars from Earth is something like looking up at the sky from the bottom of a swimming pool. Even on the clearest night, Earth's dense atmosphere screens out 30 percent of the light from any star. Air turbulence causes the stars to twinkle. Seen through a telescope, the stars seem to jump around dizzily.

With the development of satellite technology, astronomers began making plans to put a powerful telescope into orbit outside Earth's atmosphere. From such a vantage point, a telescope would have an unhindered view of our solar system—and of the galaxy beyond.

The telescope that grew out of these plans was named the Hubble Space Telescope, after the famous American astronomer Edwin P. Hubble. In 1990, the 12-ton Hubble with its 94-inch-diameter mirror was carried into space aboard a space shuttle and placed in orbit approximately 380 miles above Earth. Communication between the Hubble and its NASA command base on Earth is by means of radio waves.

Aboard the Hubble are two cameras, one for photographing large objects, the other for small objects. The Hubble also carries two spectrographs, which separate light into bands of colors, enabling scientists to determine the chemical composition of the objects observed. One spectrograph analyzes objects in or near our solar system; the other analyzes objects that are farther away.

In 1993 and again in 1997, space shuttles were sent up to "capture" the Hubble and tow it into a cargo bay where it was repaired and new equipment was installed. This new equipment allows the Hubble to photograph objects that are much greater distances away.

Among the Hubble's many amazing finds is a recently discovered galaxy that is the oldest and most distant object ever observed. The light, photographed by the Hubble, left this galaxy before our planet was formed. Sights such as these provide us with startling glimpses into the birth and development of star systems. With further study, astronomers hope to determine the size and age of the universe.

1. The Hubble Space Telescope was launched in
   a. 1957.   c. 1993.
   b. 1990.   d. 1997.

2. The word in paragraph 1 that means *disturbance* is _____
   _____.

3. The words "famous American astronomer" in paragraph 3 describe
   _____.

4. While it is not directly stated, the article suggests that
   a. stars and planets are surrounded by clouds.
   b. we still do not know very much about the stars.
   c. the stars are too dizzy to study.

5. Stars twinkle because of
   a. air turbulence.
   b. radio waves.
   c. exhaust from space shuttles.

6. On the whole, the article tells about
   a. using a swimming pool to study the stars.
   b. Edwin P. Hubble's theories.
   c. studying the universe from an orbiting telescope.

7. Which statement does this article lead you to believe?
   a. Astronauts do not like having to fix the Hubble.
   b. People now know everything there is to know about Earth.
   c. Space research may teach us more than we can now imagine.

8. Why did astronomers want to set up an orbiting telescope?
   a. It was cheaper than setting up another observatory on Earth.
   b. Space has no atmosphere.
   c. The moon would not be in the way.

9. Think about the concept for this group of articles. Which statement seems true both for the article and for the concept?
   a. Beings from distant galaxies will one day use the Hubble to contact Earth.
   b. People from Earth are not interested in distant galaxies.
   c. Someday people may travel to distant galaxies.

and five billion dollars a year, and much of that amount is the cost of rockets that can be used only once.

For years scientists have wanted a completely reusable spacecraft—one that could take off, move around in space, and return to Earth without relying on disposable rocket engines. Engineers are now working with NASA to develop a new kind of rocket engine called the aerospike. The aerospike is the first new rocket engine to be developed in more than a quarter of a century.

This rocket differs in shape from the familiar rocket with its bell-shaped nozzle. Bell-shaped rocket nozzles fire hot gases downward, driving the rocket away from the direction of the thrust. The aerospike has several nozzles arranged in two parallel rows. Gases are fired from these nozzles against curved plates to produce thrust. Aerospike engines are simpler and more efficient than earlier rockets. Their new shape will allow rocket engines to adjust to changing atmospheric pressure as spacecraft leave and reenter Earth's atmosphere. They will also enable spacecraft to take off horizontally, like an airplane, rather than vertically.

Several aerospike engines will be attached to a wedge-shaped, wingless spacecraft capable of taking off and landing on its own. Two versions of this spacecraft—the X-33 and the X-34—are being tested. The smaller X-34 is a test model, which will be able to carry up to a ton of cargo. The larger X-33, which will be able to carry much heavier loads, has been dubbed the "workhorse" of the space program for the early part of the twenty-first century.

Workhorse in Space

The multistage rockets that have carried astronauts to the moon, shuttles into space, and satellites into orbit are not very efficient. Each stage of the rocket engine drops off as soon as its fuel has been burned. This method of launching spacecraft is both expensive and wasteful.

The space shuttle was the first reusable spacecraft. However, the rockets used to launch shuttles are not reusable. The shuttle program costs NASA between three

1. Engineers are developing new spacecraft that will
   - a. have disposable fuel tanks.
   - b. have a new kind of rocket engine.
   - c. travel to other galaxies.
   - d. carry alien creatures.

2. The word in paragraph 1 that means *having more than one part* is

   _____.

3. The words "wedge-shaped" and "wingless" in paragraph 5 describe

   _____.

4. While it is not directly stated, the article suggests that
   - a. developing new rocket engines is expensive.
   - b. developing new rockets is a waste of time.
   - c. engineers know very little about how rockets work.

5. The aerospike rocket will allow spacecraft to take off
   - a. vertically.
   - b. horizontally.
   - c. backward.

6. On the whole, the article tells about
   - a. problems NASA is having with its engineers.
   - b. why making rockets out of bells is not working.
   - c. creating a completely reusable spacecraft.

7. Which statement does this article lead you to believe?
   - a. Scientists only want to perfect the rockets they have now.
   - b. Scientists have no hope of ever building an aerospike engine.
   - c. Scientists may even improve on the aerospike engine someday.

8. Why is the X-34 spacecraft smaller than the X-33?
   - a. The X-34 is a test model.
   - b. The X-34 will burn up on reentry to Earth's atmosphere.
   - c. The X-34 will have an airplane engine.

9. Think about the concept for this group of articles. Which statement seems true both for the article and for the concept?
   - a. People hope to reach the stars one day.
   - b. People have begun to reach their limits.
   - c. The stars are already too close to us.

New Medicines from the Sea

The earth's oceans, which cover 70 percent of the earth's surface, are a frontier that we are just beginning to explore. Scientists know that the undersea world is a storehouse of oil, minerals, and protein-rich foods. The oceans are also a storehouse of plants and animals. Some of these living things contain substances that can be made into useful medicines.

Scientists have long known that seawater speeds the healing of certain kinds of wounds. Medical experts believe that certain fungi floating in seawater may be responsible. One new medicine, cephalothin (sə fal'ə thən) is already being made from a fungus that floats in the Mediterranean Sea. Cephalothin kills certain germs that penicillin will not kill.

The fungus used to make cephalothin is only one of about 300 kinds of fungi in the sea. Many of these fungi have not yet been studied. Some may yield even more valuable medicines than cephalothin.

Anyone who has ever stepped on the jellyfish called the Portuguese man-of-war knows that it contains a powerful, stinging poison. Medical researchers have studied this poison. They have also studied the poisons of sea snakes, octopuses, shell animals, and sponges. In very small quantities, some of these poisons have proved useful in the treatment of diabetes, heart disease, ulcers, and spastic paralysis.

So far, only about one percent of all the sea's forms of animal life have been studied. The time required to col-

lect any one form of sea life in large quantities has held back research.

Before too many years, however, scientists will be able to work under the sea for long periods of time. They will live in structures like the Sealabs. Among these scientists will be doctors testing sea life for new and better kinds of medicines.

154

1. Cephalothin comes from a
    a. plant. c. fungus.
    b. sponge. d. fish.

2. The word in sentence 6 that means *a group of lower plants that includes molds*

    is _____ .

3. The words "which cover 70 percent of the earth's surface" in paragraph 1 des-

    cribe the earth's _____ .

4. While it is not directly stated, the article suggests that
    a. it is good for a diabetic to be stung by a jellyfish.
    b. scientists have always experimented with poisons.
    c. new attitudes about poisonous substances are developing.

5. Cephalothin comes from one of
    a. the jellyfish family.
    b. 300 kinds of fungi.
    c. 800 kinds of fungi.

6. On the whole, this article tells about
    a. the sea as a source of new medicines.
    b. using seawater to treat heart disease.
    c. stepping on fish that can sting you.

7. Which statement does this article lead you to believe?
    a. Serious exploration of the ocean is already under way.
    b. There are no frontiers left to explore.
    c. The ocean will not be explored in the near future.

8. What will make it possible for scientists to be able to work under the sea?
    a. People are learning to breathe under water for longer periods.
    b. Doctors will live in Portuguese submarines.
    c. They will live in structures like the Sealabs.

9. Think about the concept for this group of articles. Which statement seems true
    both for the article and for the concept?
    a. All our diseases will be conquered by medicines from the sea.
    b. Some diseases may disappear with the help of new sea medicines.
    c. Some diseases can never be treated by any of our doctors.

THE AMERICAN ELM

Reviving an American Icon

The American elm tree, with its soaring height and gracefully arching branches, was once a common sight throughout the eastern half of the United States. Yet by 1969, ninety percent of the American elms were dead or dying.

How did this happen? By the early 1900s, the European cousins of the American elm had contracted a fungal disease. The fungus that causes the disease was first identified in the Netherlands, which is why the disease is referred to as Dutch elm disease even though it is believed to have originated elsewhere. The fungus is spread by the elm bark beetle. Some elm logs, imported to the United States from France in 1932, were carrying both the deadly fungus and the beetles. Within a short time, the beetles had spread the fungus to American elm trees.

To fight this disease, scientists crossbred American elms with European and Asiatic elms to create a disease-resistant hybrid. But these hybrids lack the characteristic height and beauty of the American elm. Another disease-resistant elm—the Liberty

elm—was developed by genetic breeding. However, the cell structure of the Liberty elm is different from that of the American elm. Tree growers were still not satisfied.

In the late 1970s, scientists tried another plan. Here and there around the countryside a few American elm trees had survived the disease. Scientists reasoned that these trees must have a natural immunity to the Dutch elm disease. They grew cuttings from these trees and exposed them to the fungus. Some of the trees developed the disease, but two varieties—the Valley Forge elm and the New Harmony elm—developed no symptoms. Although neither variety is completely immune to the disease, both show a high level of tolerance to the fungus. After more than twenty years of research, scientists are confident that they have found a solution, if not a cure, for the problem. The Valley Forge elm and the New Harmony elm will soon replace the lost icons of the American landscape.

1. In 1932, some elm logs were imported from
   a. the United States.
   c. the Netherlands.
   b. France.
   d. Asia.

2. The word in paragraph 4 that means *not affected by a disease* is

   _____.

3. The words "soaring height and gracefully arching branches" in paragraph 1 refer to _____.

4. While it is not directly stated, the article suggests that
   a. diseases can easily travel from one country to another.
   b. very little is actually known about elm trees.
   c. the Liberty elm is the most disease-resistant tree in America.

5. The Valley Forge and New Harmony elms are varieties of
   a. American elms.
   b. European elms.
   c. Asiatic elms.

6. On the whole, the article tells about
   a. the life cycle of the elm bark beetle.
   b. a log that scientists tried to crossbreed with an elm.
   c. attempts to restore the American elm.

7. Which statement does this article lead you to believe?
   a. Americans loved their elm trees very much.
   b. The American elm was killed off by Dutch spies.
   c. We don't need elm trees in this country.

8. Why did scientists experiment with surviving American elms?
   a. Scientists thought these trees must be immune to the disease.
   b. American elms were easier to obtain than European or Asiatic elms.
   c. These trees look better in the American landscape.

9. Think about the concept for this group of articles. Which statement seems true both for the article and for the concept?
   a. It is not important to us if plants begin to die out.
   b. Plants of the future may be superior to plants we have now.
   c. Scientists try to improve on nature to prove how clever they are.

Faraway Places Just Like Home

In the past, foreign travel was costly and time-consuming. Until the jet age, it was generally only the well-to-do or the very adventurous who visited faraway places in the world.

Enormous jets, and smaller supersonic planes such as the British and French Concorde, have made foreign travel faster and less costly. As a result, Europeans casually plan weekend visits to San Francisco or Tokyo. Americans take cruises in the South Pacific and the Mediterranean. One travel expert believes that the average American will visit Europe at least fifteen times in his or her lifetime.

But as travelers reach faraway places, they are finding them more alike than they were even a few years ago. People all around the world are eating some of the same kinds of food. They are also wearing similar clothing.

Cultural differences between people are becoming less marked. Regional language differences and provincial customs will also tend to disappear, except where they are intentionally preserved by people proud of their cultural heritage.

Some experts believe that the world will eventually become bilingual or trilingual. They believe that there will be two or three international languages in use. Other experts believe that one language alone will become dominant everywhere for use in all international communications. The single international language might well be that of the first nation to begin full-time, world-wide television broadcasting relayed by a chain of orbiting communications satellites.

Television and supersonic transportation have made the world seem smaller. They are bringing far-apart peoples of the world closer together and making them more alike. At a time when foreign travel is increasing, travelers are increasingly finding foreign countries much less foreign.

1. In the past, only well-to-do or adventurous people
   a. were proud of their cultural heritage.
   c. visited foreign countries.
   b. spoke foreign languages.
   d. watched satellite television.

2. The word in paragraph 5 that means *able to speak two languages* is
   _____.

3. The words "proud of their cultural heritage" in paragraph 4 describe
   _____.

4. While it is not directly stated, the article suggests that
   a. experts predict that all Europeans will lose their customs.
   b. most people want to travel to foreign lands.
   c. Americans are the only people who travel much.

5. Provincial customs will tend to
   a. improve.
   b. flourish.
   c. disappear.

6. On the whole, the article tells about
   a. Europeans who plan weekend visits around the world.
   b. the kind of food and clothing to expect in a foreign country.
   c. the loss of cultural and language differences around the world.

7. Which statement does this article lead you to believe?
   a. Most people will be unable to speak a foreign language.
   b. People will be better able to communicate with each other.
   c. There will be many more languages in the world of tomorrow.

8. Why does the world seem smaller?
   a. Television and supersonic jets are bringing distant people together.
   b. The world begins to shrink when far-apart peoples live closer together.
   c. Orbiting communications satellites are forcing languages to die out.

9. Think about the concept for this group of articles. Which statement seems true both for the article and for the concept?
   a. International communication requires a single language.
   b. In the future, people will find it easier to understand each other.
   c. Americans will never learn a foreign language.

Taller or Smaller?

We have learned a great deal about how physical traits are passed from generation to generation. Scientists know that DNA molecules in human cells carry inherited physical traits in a sort of chemical code.

Someday we may learn how to change these DNA molecules so as to change the physical traits they carry. Eventually, parents may be able to choose what traits their children will inherit: blue eyes or brown, tall bodies or short.

Most children of today are taller than their parents, but this may be due to better nutrition rather than to an inherited change. In some population groups, height is increasing one inch per generation.

Is it a good thing for people to get taller and taller? No, say certain experts. The human skeleton would be strained carrying the weight of a very tall body. In a world where workers use power tools for heavy work, there is no special advantage in great height or strength. It might be better, some say, if people got smaller.

Smaller humans would need less food and could live in smaller houses. They would fit more comfortably into cramped spacecraft. They would drive smaller cars on narrower roads. Smaller people would make the world seem larger and less crowded. The world's natural resources would last longer. So it is possible that if scientists learn to control inherited physical traits, they might speak out for a reduction in human size.

Anthropologists have estimated the heights of ancient peoples from fossil bones. They have compared these

heights with the heights of people now living in all parts of the world. The evidence appears that most people are getting taller. The human of tomorrow may be still taller—unless he or she decides to be smaller.

160

FIND THE ANSWERS

1. One reason children today are taller than their parents may be because of better
   - a. nutrition.
   - b. DNA.
   - c. ancestors.
   - d. anthropologists.

2. The word in paragraph 1 that means *certain qualities or features* is

   _____ .

3. The words "carrying the weight of a very tall body" in paragraph 4 refer to the

   human _____ .

4. While it is not directly stated, the article suggests that
   - a. tall people must drive smaller cars.
   - b. it is always better to be taller.
   - c. there are advantages to being small.

5. Someday scientists may learn how to change
   - a. DNA molecules.
   - b. fossil bones.
   - c. nutrition.

6. On the whole, the article tells about
   - a. human strength needed for heavy work.
   - b. human height today and in the future.
   - c. anthropologists who study fossil bones.

7. Which statement does this article lead you to believe?
   - a. Scientists want to keep people small so they can be controlled.
   - b. Scientists think humans of the future should all be very tall.
   - c. Scientists may control the size of humans of the future.

8. Why are scientists able to tell the height of ancient peoples?
   - a. They can tell by looking at their pictures.
   - b. They can estimate the heights from fossil bones.
   - c. They know all old people must be quite small.

9. Think about the concept for this group of articles. Which statement seems true both for the article and for the concept?
   - a. Humans of the future may be a product of their own planning.
   - b. It is against the law to try to change your physical traits.
   - c. Humans of the future will be the tallest ever to live.

Electronic Money

Today it is possible for a person to earn money, get paid, and pay bills without handling coins, bills, or even checks. Electronic banking is what makes this possible.

Bankers know that computers can take over more of our bookkeeping and bill-paying, making cash and checks virtually unnecessary. Eventually, a nationwide network of computers will handle almost all financial transactions. Homes and businesses will be tied into this computer network just as they are now tied into the telephone network.

The new system will work something like this. Sally works at a bookstore. Every two weeks, a computer at Sally's bank transfers a credit representing Sally's salary from her employer's account to Sally's account. When Sally instructs it to, the bank's computer will then transfer smaller credits to other accounts for Sally's fixed bills, such as rent and car payments.

To purchase clothes at a department store or food at a grocery store, Sally uses a coded bank card to "pay" for her purchases. A machine at each store connects with the bank's computer. The computer then transfers money electronically from Sally's bank account directly to the store's account. Sally's purchases are paid for immediately.

Each transfer of money takes place instantly. Sally does not need to wait for a monthly bank statement or for checks to travel through the mail. When Sally gets home, she can check all her financial transactions by contacting her bank on her home computer.

Even though Sally can get along quite nicely without checks, most financial experts believe that she will still need to carry some cash for small purchases. And this will come in handy if she ever loses her bank card!

1. Each transfer of money would take place
   - a. instantly.
   - b. regularly.
   - c. by television.
   - d. by cash.

2. The word in paragraph 2 that means *nearly* or *almost* is

   _____.

3. The words "such as rent and car payments" in paragraph 3 describe

   _____.

4. While it is not directly stated, the article suggests that
   - a. Sally is a good bookkeeper.
   - b. it is always better to buy on credit.
   - c. computers make fewer mistakes than people.

5. Financial transactions are stored in the
   - a. push-button telephone.
   - b. bank's vaults.
   - c. computer's memory.

6. On the whole, the article tells about
   - a. handling coins, bills, and checks.
   - b. electronic financial transactions.
   - c. problems with Sally's bank card.

7. Which statement does this article lead you to believe?
   - a. Electronic banking is more efficient than using checks and currency.
   - b. Electronic banking will keep people out of debt.
   - c. With the disappearance of checks, stores will wait longer to be paid.

8. Why should Sally always carry some cash?
   - a. She needs it for small purchases.
   - b. She thinks it is good luck to carry it.
   - c. She likes the feel of it in her pocket.

9. Think about the concept for this group of articles. Which statement seems true both for the article and for the concept?
   - a. People will never again have to pay for the things they buy.
   - b. An electronic credit system saves time and is more accurate.
   - c. People will no longer receive salaries for their work.

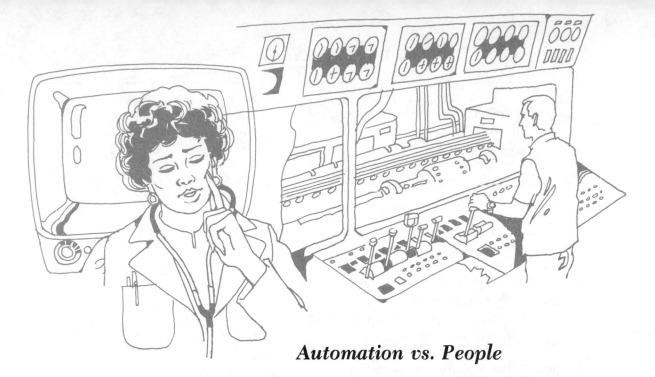

Automation vs. People

In factories and stores, in offices and on farms, new machines are taking over many jobs that used to be done by people. Today, one person operates a small factory from a single control panel. One computer takes over the tasks of dozens of office workers, while vending machines replace salesclerks in stores.

In the future, machines will continue to do even more of the world's work. Some people fear that there will not be enough work left for people to do in an age of automation. Surprisingly, however, the new machines often create new jobs. Engineers will be needed to design even better machines, while skilled technicians will be needed to install them, keep them operating, and repair them.

Fortunately, there will always be some jobs that machines cannot do. Many of these jobs have to do with helping other people.

No machine will replace doctors, nurses, and the others who help them care for sick people, for babies, and for the very old. No machine will replace the social worker or counselor who helps people in trouble. Teaching machines and television will be useful tools in the classroom, but they will not replace teachers. Machines are not likely to replace lawyers, ministers, police officers, firefighters, or day-care workers.

As newer and better machines are built, work patterns will have to change. Employees will keep going back to school to learn new skills, and this will create jobs for more teachers.

New and better machines will save time so that employees will work shorter hours. Most people will have more leisure time. This will create new jobs in businesses connected with hobbies, entertainment, and sports.

Increasing automation will create some unemployment, but it will also create new opportunities. No matter how many machines are invented, there will still be work for people to do.

164

1. Salesclerks in stores may be replaced by
   a. control panels.
   c. technicians.
   b. vending machines.
   d. supervisors.

2. The word in paragraph 2 that means *mechanical systems for doing work* is

   _____ .

3. The words "that used to be done by people" in paragraph 1 refer to

   _____ .

4. While it is not directly stated, the article suggests that
   a. people want doctors to be teaching machines.
   b. people are still more important than machines.
   c. people should be replaced by better machines.

5. As new and better machines are built, work patterns will
   a. have to change.
   b. stay the same.
   c. become less skilled.

6. On the whole, the article tells about
   a. sick people and old persons who are machines.
   b. replacing all people with much better machines.
   c. people and machines in the age of automation.

7. Which statement does this article lead you to believe?
   a. Machines will soon do all the teaching needed.
   b. No one will ever need to go to school again.
   c. Education will always be important.

8. Why will people have more leisure time?
   a. They will all be unemployed.
   b. They will work shorter hours.
   c. Machines will do all the work.

9. Think about the concept for this group of articles. Which statement seems true both for the article and for the concept?
   a. People may need skills we know nothing about in today's world.
   b. The skills people have will always be exactly as they are right now.
   c. In the future, skilled technicians will have the only good jobs.

Farms in Space

One day, manned space stations will be orbiting Earth, and astronauts will be exploring the solar system. The space stations and spacecraft will be equipped with prepackaged, dehydrated food, but for longer missions in space it will be necessary for astronauts to grow some of their own food. For proper growth, plants require nutrient-rich soil, light, and water. Transporting all these aboard a spacecraft is impractical.

An alternative farming technique is known as hydroponics. It allows farmers to grow plants without soil and can be modified to enable astronauts to farm in space. For over a century, scientists have known that plants need the nutrients found in soil; they do not need the soil itself to grow. Scientists analyzed soil to determine its chemical nutrients. When they mixed these chemicals with water, seedlings grew into healthy plants.

Hydroponic scientists have developed two different methods for growing plants without soil. One method replaces soil with an aggregate, or mixture, of sand, gravel, or planting mix. Seeds are planted in this aggregate and fed with nutrient-rich water. Another method does away with soil, or a soil substitute, altogether. In this method, plants are grown directly in water to which the nutrients have been added. Since there is nothing to support the root structure, plants grown in a water culture must be supported in some way, often in trays with holes for the roots.

Hydroponics was originally developed for use in areas on Earth with poor soil or with no soil, such as desert areas and the polar regions. By growing plants in several different combinations of nutrients, scientists are discovering the best combination for each variety of plant.

Information gathered from these experiments is being put to commercial use today, notably in vegetable farming. In the future, hydroponics will continue to be of benefit both here on Earth as food production is forced to respond to the demands of an ever-increasing population, and in space as we begin to colonize a new frontier.

1. Hydroponics was originally developed for use in areas with
    a. poor soil or no soil.
    c. rich nutrients.
    b. few farmers.
    d. space programs.

2. The word in paragraph 1 that means *from which the water has been removed* is _____.

3. The words "or mixture of sand, gravel, or planting mix" in paragraph 3 describe _____.

4. While it is not directly stated, the article suggests that
    a. astronauts may starve on long missions into deep space.
    b. there is no practical application of hydroponics.
    c. it is important to increase crop yields around the world.

5. Plants can be grown in water if the water
    a. has been dehydrated.
    b. contains the essential nutrients.
    c. contains aggregate.

6. On the whole, the article tells about
    a. farming in the desert.
    b. a useful alternative farming method.
    c. colonizing new frontiers.

7. Which statement does this article lead you to believe?
    a. Hydroponics will be of greater benefit in the future than now.
    b. Plants grow faster in aggregate than in water.
    c. American consumers will never buy hydroponic vegetables.

8. Why is hydroponics a useful farming technique for space travel?
    a. It allows plants to be grown in the dark.
    b. It allows plants to be gorwn in the dessert.
    c. It allows plants to be grown without soil.

9. Think about the concept for this group of articles. Which statement seems true both for the article and for the concept?
    a. Solutions to Earth's problems can sometimes solve problems of space exploration, and vice versa.
    b. Growing plants without soil could be dangerous.
    c. Some day space travellers won't need food.

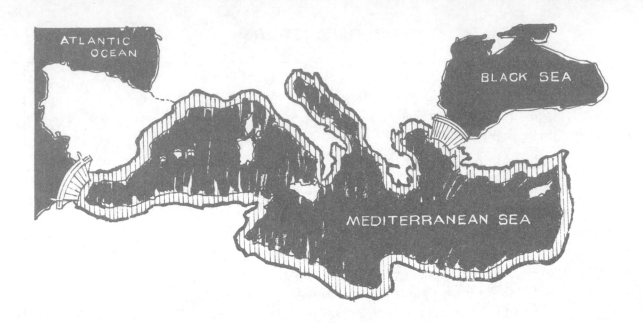

Changing a Sea into a Lake

The Mediterranean Sea was once a pair of lakes. One of the lakes was east of Italy's boot-shaped peninsula. The other was west of it. When the Ice Age ended and the continental glaciers melted, the level of the world's oceans rose. Water from the Atlantic flowed into the lakes. Many square miles of fertile land bordering the lakes disappeared underwater.

By building a dam across the Strait of Gibralter and lowering the level of the Mediterranean, people may win back this land someday. Once the Strait of Gibralter is closed off, evaporation from the surface of the Mediterranean would lower the water level by 20 to 40 inches a year. New land would appear all around the edge of the Mediterranean. The new land could provide croplands and additional living space for the crowded populations of the future.

The countries that border the Mediterranean would gain about 100,000 square miles of fertile land. Maps of Europe, Asia, and Africa would all look very different. The Mediterranean Sea would be a lake.

The project is not likely to be undertaken in the near future. Damming the Strait of Gibralter would be enormously difficult. The dam would have to be 18 miles long. It would also have to be tall and extremely strong to withstand immense pressure from the sea. The dam would have to be by-passed by a ship canal with locks. A smaller dam would be needed across the Dardanelles, east of Greece, in order to seal the Black Sea off from the Mediterranean.

Turning the Mediterranean Sea into a shrinking lake would require the close cooperation of the many different nations who would be losing their fine harbors on that body of water. They would pay with their harbors for the benefit of new farmland and living space.

168

1. The Mediterranean Sea was once a
   a. pair of lakes.   c. glacial lake.
   b. shrinking lake.   d. Greek lake.

2. The word in paragraph 1 that means *a stretch of land with water around three sides* is _____.

3. The words "across the Dardanelles, east of Greece" in paragraph 4 describe a

   _____.

4. While it is not directly stated, the article suggests that
   a. the surface of the earth keeps changing.
   b. our earth has always looked as it does now.
   c. only people can change the surface of the earth.

5. A dam across the Strait of Gibraltar would have to be
   a. 18 miles long.
   b. 100,000 miles long.
   c. smaller than the dam to seal off the Black Sea.

6. On the whole, the article tells about
   a. the crowded populations of Asia in the future.
   b. reclaiming land from the Mediterranean Sea.
   c. the origin of the Mediterranean and the Black Sea.

7. Which statement does this article lead you to believe?
   a. It is not difficult to find ways to gain more land.
   b. People are looking for ways to find more land.
   c. There is enough land on earth now to serve the future.

8. Why would different nations benefit even if they lost their fine harbors?
   a. They would gain small dams with great pressures.
   b. They would gain ship canals with many locks.
   c. They would gain farmland and living space.

9. Think about the concept for this group of articles. Which statement seems true both for the article and for the concept?
   a. Someday all the maps of the world will have to be changed.
   b. Someday all the seas will turn into evaporated surfaces.
   c. Someday people may be in need of more living space.

Running out of Steam

In the Western United States, Mexico, Italy, Iceland, and New Zealand there are huge underground reservoirs of very hot water. This water has been heated by contact with molten rock thrust up near Earth's surface by volcanic action. When a well is drilled into the water pocket, a jet of steam shoots high into the air.

Several of these enormous hot-water, or geothermal, pockets lie under California's fertile, but dry, Central Valley. It was once hoped that these reservoirs could be used to solve two of the area's problems: the need for electric power and the need for water.

Geothermal reservoirs in southern and northern California have been used to produce electricity. Steam from deep in the ground has been fed into turbines to generate electricity. However, these geothermal energy plants are running into trouble. The water used in the production of electricity was not replaced, and now the underground hot-water pockets are beginning to run dry. Steam from the world's largest geothermal energy producer, The Geysers, which is located near Santa Rosa, California, has been dropping 10 percent a year since the mid-1980s.

Meanwhile, hopes that the steam used to produce electricity could be cooled to produce water in large enough quantities for drinking and for irrigating fields have so far proved to be unfounded.

Recently, scientists have discovered a way to study underground geothermal reservoirs. Using techniques developed to study earthquakes, scientists can determine how full a reservoir is.

The same technology can help to locate new pockets of geothermal energy. But recent shutdowns of two geothermal power plants mean that Californians must continue to look elsewhere for their electricity and water.

1. In California several geothermal pockets lie under the fertile but dry
   a. Mexican desert.
   c. Central Valley.
   b. Geysers.
   d. coastal mountains.

2. The word in paragraph 2 that means *bearing crops* is

   _____.

3. The words "the world's largest geothermal energy producer" in paragraph 3
   refer to _____.

4. While it is not directly stated, the article suggests that
   a. some states need more water than they have.
   b. all states have more than enough water now.
   c. states should take water away from each other.

5. Underground water reaches Earth's surface in the form of
   a. electricity.
   b. steam jets.
   c. mineral water.

6. On the whole, the article tells about problems with
   a. using underground reservoirs for production of electricity and water.
   b. the farmers who live in California.
   c. the turbines of electric power generators.

7. Which statement does this article lead you to believe?
   a. California's need for water will drop over the next twenty years.
   b. California doesn't need much electricity.
   c. There is no easy solution to California's need for water and electricity.

8. Why do scientists study underground reservoirs using earthquake technology?
   a. California has a lot of earthquakes.
   b. Scientists don't want earthquakes to destroy the power plants.
   c. They want to know how full the reservoirs are and to locate new ones.

9. Think about the concept for this group of articles. Which statement seems true
   both for the article and for the concept?
   a. It is not possible to take water from underground reservoirs in Italy.
   b. Huge underground reservoirs are located only in southern California.
   c. For underground reservoirs to be useful, we must learn how to
      replace them.

Sharing Antarctica

The International Geophysical Year (IGY)—July 1, 1957 to December 31, 1958—was a time set aside by sixty-six nations for study of Earth and its environment. A major part of the IGY had to do with research projects in Antarctica. Few scientists had ever worked in Antarctica, so little was known about that continent.

During the IGY, scientists from twelve nations worked in Antarctica. Geologists recorded earthquakes, mapped mountains, and took samples of rocks. Meteorologists measured winds and temperatures. They learned how weather at the south pole affects weather in other places.

For the benefit of science, the nations that had previously claimed parts of Antarctica set aside their claims. Boundary lines marked on maps of Antarctica were ignored. Scientists were free to go where they pleased and to set up stations wherever research was needed. They were free to visit stations set up by other nations and to exchange information.

This experiment in scientific cooperation among nations was so successful that it led to a new kind of treaty. The Antarctic Treaty, signed in 1959 by these twelve nations, made Antarctica a free area that could be used only for peaceful purposes. However, because they want control over mineral rights, seven of those nations are now claiming parts of Antarctica. The United States and the other four nations do not recognize these claims.

Since the establishment of the treaty, several other countries have joined and set up research of their own. The treaty nations have agreed to protect Antarctica's animals and plants and to delay settlement of land claims. It is possible that Antarctica will always be a free area. It may be the first of many areas where people of different nations work together for the benefit of all.

172

FIND THE ANSWERS

1. A major part of the IGY had to do with research projects in
   - a. Australia.
   - b. Antarctica.
   - c. Washington.
   - d. the Arctic.

2. The words in paragraph 3 that mean *the borders of something* are

   _____ _____.

3. The words "free area" in paragraph 4 refer to _____.

4. While it is not directly stated, the article suggests that
   - a. meteorologists were the only persons free to go where they pleased.
   - b. scientists from Antarctica went to twelve nations.
   - c. The nations were pleased with the results of their experiment.

5. Antarctica was made a free area by the terms of the
   - a. Antarctic Treaty.
   - b. International Geophysical Year.
   - c. United States of America.

6. On the whole, the article tells about
   - a. an experiment in scientific cooperation.
   - b. Earth and its environment marked on maps.
   - c. meteorologists who measure temperatures.

7. Which statement does this article lead you to believe?
   - a. Geologists and meteorologists are not really scientists anymore.
   - b. Scientists think all scientific knowledge should be kept secret.
   - c. Scientists are glad to share their knowledge with each other.

8. Why was so little known about the icy continent?
   - a. No one knew where the boundaries were.
   - b. Few scientists had ever worked there.
   - c. Dangerous beasts kept people away from the shores.

9. Think about the concept for this group of articles. Which statement seems true both for the article and for the concept?
   - a. Someday all peoples may cooperate in more and more fields.
   - b. Someday all peoples of the world will become scientists.
   - c. Someday all peoples may fight over the icy continents.

173

Games Mathematicians Play

There are many similarities between business competition and a card game such as bridge or poker. In each case both sides want to win. Neither side can learn all the secrets of the other side. Poker players can only guess what cards their opponents hold. A manufacturer can only guess what new products a competitor is bringing out.

The outcome of any competition depends partly on luck. It also depends on strategies the competitors use. Both the poker player and the manufacturer must make decisions based on their guesses about what their opponents will do next. Each must understand that the other might be bluffing.

It took a mathematician to translate this kind of competition into numbers and formulas and create a new branch of mathematics called Game Theory. The creator of Game Theory was John Von Neumann, who also helped to develop the atomic bomb.

Von Neumann's Game Theory makes a card game serve as a mathematical model of a real-life problem such as business competition. Mathematicians analyze the moves that a player can make. They also analyze the moves the opponent can make. They can then advise the businesses on their best strategy. They may even be able to predict the outcome of the "game."

Game Theory is used today to predict ups and downs in the nation's economy and to advise manufacturers when to bring out a new product. In years to come, Game Theory may be used to attack social problems that involve competition.

There is even a chance that Game Theory could eliminate war by providing a framework for discussion between nations in disagreement. Mathematicians who play games may prove to be the peacemakers of tomorrow's world.

1. The peacemakers of tomorrow's world may be
    a. opponents.
    c. business people.
    b. mathematicians.
    d. manufacturers.

2. The word in sentence 4 that means *one who is on the opposite side in a game* is

    _____ .

3. The words "a new branch of mathematics" in paragraph 3 refer to the

    _____ _____ .

4. While it is not directly stated, the article suggests that
    a. wars are one stage in the competition between nations.
    b. a game can cause wars between many nations.
    c. social problems are too difficult for mathematics.

5. John Von Neumann also helped to develop the
    a. game of bridge.
    b. way to bluff.
    c. atomic bomb.

6. On the whole, the article tells about
    a. the difference between a card game and business competition.
    b. a new branch of mathematics that can be used in many ways.
    c. manufacturers who must make decisions about their competitors.

7. Which statement does the article lead you to believe?
    a. The Game Theory could be used in many different areas.
    b. Only manufacturers are allowed to use the Game Theory.
    c. The Game Theory will be used like a weapon in an attack.

8. Why are there similarities between business competition and card games?
    a. Both sides want to win.
    b. Neither side can keep secrets.
    c. Both sides use mathematics.

9. Think about the concept for this group of articles. Which statement seems true both for the article and for the concept?
    a. A card game cannot serve as a model of real-life problems.
    b. Mathematicians are too limited to advise business on strategy.
    c. Planning and good sense may rule the world one day.

The Speed-Up
That Will Slow Time

Albert Einstein's famous Theory of Relativity states that time, like height, width, and breadth, is a dimension. These four dimensions are not fixed and unchangeable. They change as speed of movement changes. The only measurement in the universe that is fixed and unchangeable is the speed of light in a vacuum. That speed is 186,281 miles per second.

According to Einstein's theory, when the speed of a moving object increases, the object shrinks and becomes heavier. For the object, time passes more slowly. At speeds achieved in the past, these changes were too small to be noticeable.

At the greatest speeds achieved today, the changes are still very small. A jet plane traveling 1,400 miles per hour is only ten billionths of an inch shorter than the same plane on the ground. A clock aboard an artificial satellite traveling five miles per second loses only one hundredth of a second per year compared to a clock on the earth's surface.

It is only when a moving object approaches the speed of light that fantastic things happen. At 93,000 miles per second a 20-foot-long spacecraft would shrink to 17 feet. Aboard a spacecraft speeding toward the stars at 160,000 miles per second, time would pass just half as fast as time passes on earth. Two years on the spacecraft would be equal to four years on the earth's surface.

What an adventure awaits the astronauts of the future! They may travel so fast that shapes and measurements change. Even stranger, time will slow down.

Albert Einstein was a bold adventurer in the world of mathematics. From his views of the relationship between space and time came the knowledge that will help people explore distant planets and stars.

FIND THE ANSWERS

1. The speed of light in a vacuum is
      a. 222,246 miles per hour.   c. 281,186 miles per second.
      b. 100,000 miles per hour.   d. 186,281 miles per second.

2. The word in paragraph 1 that means *a measurement of time, breadth, width, or height* is _____.

3. The words "a bold adventurer in the world of mathematics" in paragraph 6 describe _____ _____.

4. While it is not directly stated, the article suggests that
      a. the speed of light has no effect on measurements.
      b. the only way we travel is at the speed of light.
      c. we cannot yet travel at the speed of light.

5. When the speed of a moving object increases, the object
      a. stretches and becomes stronger.
      b. shrinks and becomes heavier.
      c. swells and becomes lighter.

6. On the whole, the article tells about
      a. the relationship between speed and time.
      b. shapes and measurements that keep changing.
      c. clocks aboard an artificial satellite.

7. Which statement does this article lead you to believe?
      a. Time passes twice as fast on earth as it does in space.
      b. Time passes the same way for all, in space or on earth.
      c. Future astronauts will not age as quickly as people on earth.

8. Why were Einstein's views of space and time important?
      a. They helped people learn about the speed of light.
      b. They gave people the chance to build moving objects.
      c. They gave people the knowledge to make space travel possible.

9. Think about the concept for this group of articles. Which statement seems true both for the article and for the concept?
      a. People are beginning to plan further travel into space.
      b. Most people agree that our spacecraft will be too short for high speeds.
      c. Albert Einstein was the world's finest spacecraft designer.

Say Goodby to Traffic Jams

Today, transportation is one of the major problems of large cities. Rush hours often create huge traffic jams. Exhaust fumes from thousands of automobiles pollute the air. In hopes of solving these problems, some scientists and engineers are considering new ways of transportation for the city of the future.

In tomorrow's city, people may travel short distances of a mile or less on a transporter belt or "moving walk." Passengers will be able to walk on and off at any point just as safely as people today step on and off an escalator.

Tomorrow's automobile may be changed greatly from today's models. It might be small and square and run on electric batteries, which will produce little noise and no fumes. However, most people will no longer own their own cars. Instead, they will ride in self-service taxicabs stationed underground at different points along a city's main thoroughfares. To unlock the door of one, people will put a credit card into a slot. To go to the suburbs, they will drive the cab themselves. To travel about in the city, they will simply tell a computer station where they want to go. Then, an automatic driving system will move them to their destination.

In the city of the future, many people may travel on a very fast underground train. Perhaps they will ride in electronically controlled "pods" that run on monorails. These "pods" could carry people from their homes to any destination they wish.

For people in the cities of tomorrow, traffic jams and exhaust fumes will be a thing of the past.

1. Tomorrow's automobile may be
   - a. large and round.
   - b. small and square.
   - c. little and pointed.
   - d. wide and triangular.

2. The word in paragraph 1 that means *make dirty or unclean* is

   _____ .

3. The words "stationed underground at different points along a city's main

   thoroughfares" in paragraph 3 refer to _____ .

4. While it is not directly stated, the article suggests that
   - a. transporter belts will be very dangerous to use.
   - b. people will no longer be able to go where they wish.
   - c. traveling in the future may be more pleasant.

5. People of the future may travel
   - a. by more automatic means.
   - b. in self-service "pads."
   - c. only by underground trains.

6. On the whole, the article tells about
   - a. exhaust fumes in huge traffic jams.
   - b. transportation in the city of the future.
   - c. people who must travel underground.

7. Which statement does this article lead you to believe?
   - a. Computers of the future will do less work than those of today.
   - b. Computers can be used only for figuring out traffic patterns.
   - c. Driving could be safer when it is controlled by computers.

8. Why would a person put his credit card into a slot?
   - a. In order to drive the electronic "pad."
   - b. In order to unlock the door of the self-service taxicab.
   - c. In order to store the credit card until it is needed.

9. Think about the concept for this group of articles. Which statement seems true both for the article and for the concept?
   - a. Huge traffic jams and exhaust fumes will always be a problem in our cities.
   - b. Cities of the future could be cleaner than they are today.
   - c. The best idea might be to eliminate cities entirely.

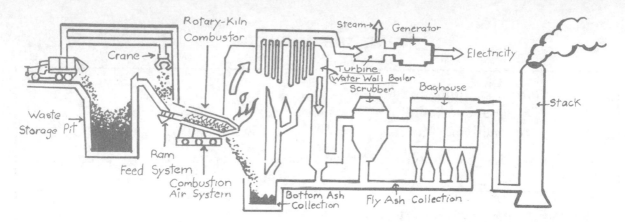

The diagram shows labeled parts: Crane, Rotary-Kiln Combustor, Steam, Generator, Electricity, Turbine, Water Wall Boiler, Scrubber, Baghouse, Stack, Waste Storage Pit, Ram, Feed System, Combustion Air System, Bottom Ash Collection, Fly Ash Collection

The Three R's for the Next Millennium—Reduce, Reuse, Recycle

Ever since the city of Athens, Greece established the first municipal garbage dump in 500 B.C., we have been looking for ways to dispose of our garbage. Recently, there has been a growing awareness of the need to reuse, recycle, and reduce our waste materials.

In the past, Americans threw away vast quantities of valuable substances. It was cheaper for manufacturers to buy new raw materials than to reclaim used ones. But today many natural resources are being used up. Recycling and reusing will solve not just one problem, but three. They will provide new supplies of substances like metals, help preserve the world's natural resources, and dispose of a good deal of the garbage we produce.

Yet even with reuse and recycling, cities still have to deal with mountains of garbage every day. This garbage has often been buried in landfills, but many cities are running out of land. As the population grows, this land will be needed for homes, businesses, and farms. Clearly, we need to reduce the amount of garbage we have to dispose of.

Until the late 1970s, garbage and lawn clippings were burned in backyard incin-erators to reduce their volume. The passage of the Clean Air Act put an end to most of this open-air burning. Today, many cities and towns reduce their garbage by burning it in waste-to-energy (WTE) incinerators, which reduce the amount of waste sent to landfills by 70 to 90 percent. As an added bonus, this process produces much-needed electricity.

The most common WTE system is the mass burn incinerator. In this type of incinerator, garbage is dumped into a large pit. Then cranes lift it into hoppers that carry it to the furnace to burn. The furnace heats a boiler which turns water into steam. The steam, in turn, powers a generator which produces electricity. Leftover ash is hauled away to be used in landfills or in construction. To control toxic fumes, incinerator emissions are carefully monitored and filtered.

By the mid-1990s, approximately 17 percent of the garbage in the United States was being processed in WTE systems, and that number is increasing every year. The battle for a cleaner, healthier environment isn't over, but with reuse, recycling, and reduction, we can already see real improvement.

1. Many towns and cities are using garbage to produce
   - a. a vast trash heap.
   - b. clean air.
   - c. electricity.
   - d. incinerators.

2. The word in paragraph 4 that means *places for burning* is

   _____.

3. The words "needed for homes, businesses, and farms" in paragraph 3 refer to

   _____.

4. While it is not directly stated, the article suggests that
   - a. electricity produced by burning garbage is unclean.
   - b. disposing of garbage is becoming a serious problem.
   - c. the world's natural resources will never be in danger.

5. The most common waste-to-energy system is the
   - a. mass burn incinerator.
   - b. Clean Air Act.
   - c. municipal dump of Athens, Greece.

6. On the whole, the article tells about
   - a. why manufacturers bought raw materials.
   - b. turning electricity into garbage.
   - c. the need to reuse, recycle, and reduce garbage.

7. Which statement does this article lead you to believe?
   - a. Electricity produced by burning garbage is less expensive.
   - b. In the future, there will be stronger laws to enforce recycling.
   - c. There is no market for recycled metals.

8. Why did manufacturers prefer to buy new raw materials?
   - a. It was cheaper.
   - b. There was not enough garbage.
   - c. Garbage was too messy to sort through.

9. Think about the concept for this group of articles. Which statement seems true both for the article and for the concept?
   - a. The only thing to do with garbage is to bury it.
   - b. There will never be any profit from recycled garbage.
   - c. People will invent new uses for garbage in the years to come.

Art—But What Kind?

There may be an art explosion ahead.

People will be working shorter hours, taking longer vacations, and retiring at an earlier age. They will have more time, and probably more money, for activities not directly connected with making a living. Under these circumstances, many people will take a great interest in art.

What kind of art might the future bring? The questions can't be answered with certainty. Art is always a product of its own time and it changes as life changes.

It is possible, however, that the future will bring a new appreciation for the art of the past. In an age of mass production and synthetic materials, people may place a higher value on handicrafts, things created by hand from natural materials. People may want to see pictures that suggest an "old-fashioned" kind of beauty which has become rare in the world they know.

It is also possible that in the future much of the art we know today will disappear. New art forms may be so exciting and full of motion that no one will want to look at a flat picture or a sculpture that stands still.

It is certain that tomorrow's artists will use new substances in new ways. The unusual materials are likely to be combined with elements that were once thought of as separate. Light patterns will combine with sound. Color and form will combine with motion. These elements will reach out and surround the viewers. They won't just *look* at art; they will experience it.

What new kind of beauty will tomorrow's artists create? The people who know most about art forms and the history of art will only predict that there will be new and surprising things.

1. In the future, artists may combine color and form with
   a. natural materials.
   b. synthetics.
   c. the viewer.
   d. motion.

2. The word in the last paragraph that means *tell in advance* is

   _____ .

3. The words "a product of its own time" in paragraph 3 describe

   _____ .

4. While it is not directly stated, the article suggests that
   a. all artists paint the same way today.
   b. art of the past is still admired.
   c. no one likes "old-fashioned" art.

5. People may place a higher value on
   a. handicrafts.
   b. synthetic materials.
   c. flat pictures.

6. On the whole, the article tells about
   a. the changing world of art.
   b. sculptures that move.
   c. new materials in history.

7. Which statement does this article lead you to believe?
   a. Handicrafts will be the only true art of the future.
   b. It is easy to predict the art forms and materials of the future.
   c. Artists will need to know more than how to paint and carve.

8. Why will viewers "experience" art someday?
   a. Everyone will be given materials to create their own art.
   b. The elements of color, form, and motion will surround him.
   c. Art will be required in all public schools.

9. Think about the concept for this group of articles. Which statement seems true both for the article and for the concept?
   a. Not everyone will be pleased with the world of the future.
   b. Tomorrow's artists will only create art in a computer.
   c. It is always easy to understand new art forms.

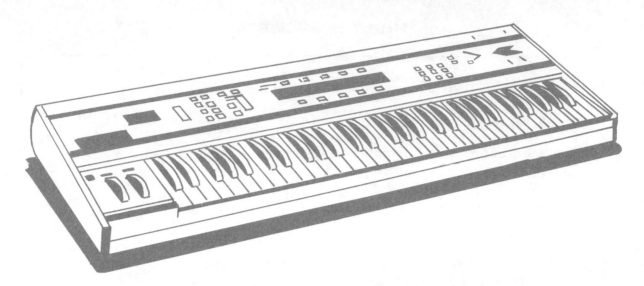

A Musical Revolution

An electronic synthesizer looks something like a cross between a piano and a computer. It has a piano keyboard, switches, flashing lights and dangling wires, and bears little resemblance to what we think of as a traditional musical instrument. Yet it can produce sounds like those of a flute, a violin, or a human voice. It can also produce unique sounds that are not at all like human voices or ordinary musical instruments.

Within the electronic synthesizer are devices that produce a changing electronic current. This current is translated into sounds that are changed in different ways by filters and volume controls. The sound is recorded on tape, after which it may be played again so that more sounds can be added. Other effects can be produced by playing the tape faster to raise the pitch of the sound, or slower to lower the pitch.

The history of the synthesizer goes back to the early twentieth century, when musicians first began experimenting with electronic sounds. However, it was not until 1940 and the invention of the tape recorder that electronic music as we think of it today became possible. The tape recorder allowed electronic sounds to be combined. By the early 1950s, musicians were experimenting with music that was not only electronically handled but also electronically produced, and in 1955 the electronic synthesizer was invented.

The electronic synthesizer gives composers command of the entire range of tones that the human ear can hear. But human musicians cannot play this music on traditional instruments.

It is not difficult to imagine the controversy that surrounded early synthesizer music. Its critics claimed that it wasn't "real" music, that no music lover would listen to it, and that people who composed for the synthesizer were not "true" musicians. Today however, electronic music is accepted and loved around the world. It is played alone and in combination with traditional instruments everywhere from rock bands to movie soundtracks to the concert stage.

1. An electronic synthesizer has
    a. synthetic wires.
    b. vacuum tubes.
    c. a limited range.
    d. keys like a piano.

2. The word in paragraph 5 that means *dispute* is _____.

3. The words "like those of a flute, a violin, or a human voice" in paragraph 1 refer to _____.

4. While it is not directly stated, the article suggests that
    a. some composers find the electronic synthesizer a challenge.
    b. at first, musicians hated the synthesizer.
    c. synthesizers cannot produce as great a range of tones as the violin.

5. Electronic music, as we know it today, was not possible until
    a. the invention of the keyboard.
    b. the invention of the tape recorder.
    c. the invention of volume controls.

6. On the whole, the article tells about
    a. music produced by an electronic instrument.
    b. the importance of music in our lives.
    c. musicians who play several instruments.

7. Which statement does this article lead you to believe?
    a. People are willing to listen to new sounds.
    b. Classical music is rarely played today.
    c. Music composers are more popular than performers.

8. Why is the sound recorded on tape?
    a. It can help the composers remember what they wrote.
    b. It can be played again and more sounds added.
    c. It can be used to direct a hundred musicians.

9. Think about the concept for this group of articles. Which statement seems true both for the article and for the concept?
    a. Music of tomorrow may no longer be music as we know it now.
    b. All music from now on will be composed on switchboards.
    c. Flashing lights and dangling wires are piano keys.

Fill in your record chart after each test. Beside the page numbers, put a one for each correct question. Put zero in the box of each question you missed. At the far right, put your total. Nine is a perfect score for each test.

When you finish all the tests in a concept, total your scores by question. The highest possible score for each question in one concept is the number of stories.

When you have taken several tests, check to see which question you get right each time. Which ones are you missing? Find the places where you need help. For example, if you are missing Question 3 often, ask for help in learning to use directing words.

As you begin each concept, copy the chart onto lined paper. Down the left side are the test page numbers. Across the top are the question numbers and the kinds of questions. For example, each Question 1 in this book asks you to recall a fact. Your scores for each question show how well you are learning each skill.

Your Reading Scores
Concept I

Question / Page 15	1 fact	2 vocabulary	3 modification	4 inference	5 fact	6 main idea	7 inference	8 cause and effect	9 concept recognition	Total for Page
17										
19										
21										
23										
25										
27										
29										
31										
33										
35										
37										
39										
41										
43										
45										
47										
49										
51										
53										
Totals by question										

Your Reading Scores

Concept III

Question	fact (1)	vocabulary (2)	modification (3)	inference (4)	fact (5)	main idea (6)	inference (7)	cause and effect (8)	concept recognition (9)	Total for Page
Page 103										
105										
107										
109										
111										
113										
115										
117										
119										
121										
123										
125										
127										
129										
131										
133										
135										
137										
139										
141										
Totals by question										

Your Reading Scores

Concept II

Question	fact (1)	vocabulary (2)	modification (3)	inference (4)	fact (5)	main idea (6)	inference (7)	cause and effect (8)	concept recognition (9)	Total for Page
Page 59										
61										
63										
65										
67										
69										
71										
73										
75										
77										
79										
81										
83										
85										
87										
89										
91										
93										
95										
97										
Totals by question										

Your Reading Scores

Concept IV

Question	fact 1	vocabulary 2	modification 3	inference 4	fact 5	main idea 6	inference 7	cause and effect 8	concept recognition 9	Total for Page
Page 147										
149										
151										
153										
155										
157										
159										
161										
163										
165										
167										
169										
171										
173										
175										
177										
179										
181										
183										
185										
Totals by question										